God's Fingerprints

God's Fingerprints

Evidence for the Christian God Is All Around
All of Us All of the Time

SECOND EDITION

Trevor Watts

WIPF & STOCK · Eugene, Oregon

GOD'S FINGERPRINTS
Evidence for the Christian God Is All Around All of Us All of the Time
Second Edition

Copyright © 2013 Trevor Watts. All rights reserved. Except for brief quotations in critical publications or reviews, no part of this book may be reproduced in any manner without prior written permission from the publisher. Write: Permissions, Wipf and Stock Publishers, 199 W. 8th Ave., Suite 3, Eugene, OR 97401.

Wipf & Stock
An Imprint of Wipf and Stock Publishers
199 W. 8th Ave., Suite 3
Eugene, OR 97401
www.wipfandstock.com

ISBN 13: 978-1-62032-820-0
Manufactured in the U.S.A.

Scripture quotations taken from the HOLY BIBLE, NEW INTERNATIONAL VERSION. Copyright © 1973,1978, 1984 by International Bible Society. Used by permission.

All royalties from the sale of this work are donated to the charity Tearfund (www.tearfund.org)

To my lovely wife, our three delightful daughters, and their families, in honor of the loving super-person who has given us life

Always be prepared to give an answer to everyone
who asks you to give the reason for the hope that you have.

1 PET 3:15

Contents

Reviews of the First Edition ix
Preface to Second Edition xi
Preface to First Edition xiii
Prologue: Clearly Perceived? xv

Part A—Tools and constraints: fingerprint powder 1

1 Bias 3
    We all have bias, so let us start there!

2 Why it matters what we believe 15
    Simply in order to live, we have answered certain questions by implication, consciously or unconsciously

3 Where do I begin? 21
    What are the simplest aspects of our experience?

4 What can I trust? 29
    Trust and its relationship to our values

5 Limits: space and time 34
    What are the implications of being limited?

6 The framework and the flesh 40
    The importance of understanding the universe we live in

7 Reason: what is it? 49
    The effects of reason on naïve experience

8 Experience: how do I understand it? 55
    The effects of experience on our reasoning

Part B—Phenomena of naïve experience: the fingerprints 63

9 Something or nothing? 65
    The something which is there, and its complexity

Contents

10 Order and chaos 74
   The existence of order suggests that true chaos does not exist

11 Sequence and consequence 80
   Causes and effects, including one miracle

12 Identity and personality 87
   Uniqueness and personhood

13 Communications? 96
   Communication and information point outside the universe

Part C—From fingerprints to identification 107

14 Origins 109
   Our experience argues for a super-personal creator

15 Possibilities 117
   Naïve experience leads us to a particular type of religion and the prime contender is Christianity

16 Purity and profanity 128
   Morals depend on something real outside the universe

17 Listen . . . is there anyone there? 137
   Reason and experience tell us to listen out for something like Christianity

18 The step which matters 146
   A summary of the argument, and the nature of Christian conversion

19 Why choose? 156
   The matter of responsibility to God

20 Truth and falsehood 162
   Truth and consistency in the Bible

21 Right and wrong 180
   Why loving God is the true basis for morality

Epilogue: Alpha and Omega 195
Bibliography 199
Subject/Name Index 203

Reviews of the First Edition

God's Fingerprints

Michael Baughen, formerly Bishop of Chester, UK:

"I am thankful to the author for writing this excellent book. It has his own particular style of carrying the reader on from one section to the next and makes some excellent arguments for the faith and exposures of the atheist positions.

The story of the miracle is stunning and handled in a perfectly balanced way."

Irving Hexham, Professor of Religious Studies, University of Calgary, Canada:

"This is an excellent and very readable book on Christian apologetics. The author is a well-respected British dental research scholar who was a consultant in periodontology at the world-renowned Guy's Hospital in London, UK. He is also a past president of the British Society of Periodontology.

The book, which proceeds in a logical manner, makes fascinating reading. Throughout the author refers to scientific indicators that raise serious questions about a purely materialist account of the world.

Refreshingly the book is free from the usual preoccupations of American Christian tracts that hammer away at the same issues again and again. Here is a new approach that is of interest to both committed Christians, atheists, and agnostics because of its engaging manner that mirrors C.S. Lewis.

This is a book I highly recommend."

Reviews of the First Edition

K.A Kitchen, Emeritus Professor of Egyptology, University of Liverpool, UK:

"What are we? Where are we, in the whole span of the set-up of our lives, as we live them, as we look around us? What (or who?) is the ultimate reality? Are we simply a flea-circus on a minor planet spinning on through a bleak void to the universe's final demise? Or in fact, are it and we the cherished creation of the ultimate Unseen Power who created humanity to share (if we are willing) in a destiny far beyond our greatest vision? What visible features (and even, available documentation) may guide us in our quest to discover the final answer?

Dr. Watts here presents his investigation with patience and engaging clarity, checking out the basic "nuts and bolts" of our situation (in all senses), step by step, by steady, relaxed and impeccable reasoning in and around all the major possibilities (and impossibilities!), reaching the conclusion via data of all kinds, that— ultimately—there is indeed a palpable "Unseen Power," who has, in fact, already "shown his hand" visibly and with great clarity in and through Jesus Christ, for all the basic matters of life and beyond it.

This book is not abstruse, but clear and patient, engaging with the wide variety of views espoused by humans, not simply pushing a single line; but it indicates clearly where the overall facts appear to lead—to God Himself, our greatest carer[1], not only a distant final judge."

---

1. equivalent US term: caregiver.

Preface to Second Edition

THE NEED FOR A new edition was borne out by the advice of numerous friends. Yes, they said, the book was definitely worth reading, but the second hundred pages were easier to read than the first hundred!

Therefore, I have listened to them! I have scrupulously gone through the first edition, and tried to enhance readability. I have also added an entirely new chapter about bias at the beginning. For those who want more references, I have supplied some.

Most reviewers have been accurate and very kind in their remarks. However, one highly critical reviewer even complained that the chapters were not numbered! Obviously he did not read the book carefully, and I have not changed much in respect of his other comments!

Trevor Watts, 2013

Preface to First Edition

My first book was in the field of evidence-based dentistry. It was a book aimed at graduates and postgraduate students to help them understand some of the evidence for practice in my specialty, periodontics, and how to assess it.

I now find that my second book is about evidence-based theology and philosophy. It is a matter of importance to all of us that our basic ideas—about who we are and what sort of universe we live in—are as correct as we can make them.

For those who do not believe in any kind of supreme being, it is important to check things out. The worst case scenario for them would be to find an existence after death for which they were not prepared, and it would be a tragedy for them to encounter a God who showed them how wrong they had been to ignore him.

For those of us who do believe in a supreme being, it is clearly important to make sure that our ideas fit the real world, and that we are not simply inventing a God to suit ourselves.

I have tried, therefore, to cover the most basic evidence which suggests to us that God is there and that he is a particular kind of God who has made himself known in a special way.

Whatever the beliefs of different readers, I would invite them to read this little offering and make their own decisions about its possible application to their lives. I hope that my views are acceptable to all Christians, that is, those who believe that Jesus is the second person of a super-personal three-in-one God, and that he died on the cross to pay the cost of our disobedience, and rose again to physical life, thereby showing he had power over death.

I also ask readers to pardon me for any errors and omissions in this text, which is a human production and therefore certain to be imperfect in some ways.

Trevor Watts, 2008

Prologue

Clearly Perceived?

The wrath of God is being revealed from heaven against all the godlessness and wickedness of men who suppress the truth by their wickedness, since what may be known about God is plain to them, because God has made it plain to them. For since the creation of the world God's invisible qualities—his eternal power and divine nature—have been clearly seen, being understood from what has been made, so that men are without excuse. For although they knew God, they neither glorified him as God nor gave thanks to him, but their thinking became futile and their foolish hearts were darkened. (Rom 1:18–21, NIV.)

ALMOST SINCE I BECAME a Christian at the age of 16, I have been impressed with the force of the above statement. St Paul was one of the outstanding thinkers of his time, and his contribution to the Christian Bible is unparalleled by the work of any other early Christian. Why was he so strong in his forthright condemnation? According to him, the creation itself is a pointer to God, and not just any god, but the God revealed in the Jewish scriptures (of which Paul was a highly educated interpreter).

The result of leaving God out of consideration is to become "futile in thinking"; as Paul sees it, accepting the Creator is essential to understanding the creation. There are many who have realized this and written of the Christian approach to nature and the Biblical view of human beings as made in God's image. But it seems to me that a further issue is raised by Paul's words. He says that those who do not honor God because of his creation are *without excuse*. They should know the Author from his work.

I am just another ordinary Christian who believes the Christian gospel is directed towards all people, and tries to put it into practice. I certainly do not claim infallibility. Rather, I would like readers to explore whether they have a similar experience of reality, and to see if my conclusions are justified. People rarely become Christians by argument, but objective truth is important to us all, whatever the dictates of the fashions of political correctness. One of my recurring thoughts is that real truth is not a matter of consensus but has objective reference points outside human opinion.

Since the basic experience of all human beings contains certain aspects which are common to everyone, we might expect broad agreement over many aspects of life, and perhaps over the question of what life is and what our lives are about. However, nothing is farther from the world we experience around us! Human beings have an amazing variety of beliefs about the universe and how they should behave in it. From this variety of beliefs springs all the conflicts which affect humankind. What one person loves in the deepest way possible, another hates with all the venom and bitterness which can be summoned.

Nothing is more apparent than that human beings are obsessed with their experience. Possessions, sex, drugs, power—these are a few of the matters on which they spend most of their time. How is it that they end up with such a diversity of beliefs? The militant atheist who is determined to attack all beliefs identified as religious, the Islamic fundamentalist who believes that he will have a gift of 70 virgins in paradise as a reward for brutally killing anyone who is "kuffar," and the determined postmodernist who believes that all conflicting human beliefs are somehow to be reconciled—these are but three examples of such diversity.

Human beliefs are arguable at every level. Where we might consider there is broad agreement—over some matters of science, for instance—there may be rancorous disagreement. In a world with myriad people, it seems that no two will be found who can agree on everything. No marriage is without arguments! Consequently, truth is not by consensus, neither is there any consensus over how human beings should behave. From these two facts come the whole of human strife and turmoil. This small book is an attempt to address the problem.

PART A

Tools and constraints: fingerprint powder

How do we show up the fingerprints we wish to identify? They need to be highlighted with a suitable powder so they can be photographed. In this first section, we shall look at what life presents to us, and a way in which we can approach the questions posed by the very simplest aspects of our experience. We shall see that both reason and experience are central to our understanding and activity. We shall also explore some of the ways in which we are limited.

Most of us approach the real world we live in, carrying a huge intellectual baggage of which we are largely unaware. For instance, we may think that it is good to be objective, to use science, and to be skeptical of anything which does not fit our views of the world. Or we may think it is good to be open to anything which claims to be helpful, no matter how preposterous it might seem.

One way of trying to avoid too much of this baggage is by scrupulously examining the most basic things we encounter, seeing where our experience leads without trying to force it into preconceived ideas.

The idea of naïve experience—with as few categories as possible, or providing its own categories—is a good starting point if we do not wish to be overwhelmed by the possible distortions built into experience by our lifelong interactions with reality. The idea came from twentieth century Dutch Calvinist philosophers, and seems very attractive to me.

I disagree with the fashionable views of postmodernism just as much as with positivism, and indeed with many approaches to philosophy. I believe that we must start thinking as a response to what is there, and that our philosophies are useless if they are not understandable to all normal adults. The great questions of knowledge and behavior cannot be answered without reference to the real world which we experience. They must start with that experience and explain it in a sensible way, or we are truly lost.

1

Bias

We all have bias, so let us start there!

Everyone has a bias. What has brought this home to me is the way in which some people, particularly those who claim to be atheists, stress that they are without bias! They make the assumption that there is a neutral way of approaching life, and then assume that that way is what they follow. How wrong they are! Let us take a moment to look at this.

Are atheists merely irrational, or are they mystics?

First, what is the basis for being an atheist? What evidence is there that atheism is true? How can we be sure there is no god, either inside or outside the universe? Plainly there is only one way: we need total knowledge of everything inside *and outside* of the universe. Only then will we know enough to be able to say definitely that there is no god, always provided that we do not find something to alter that opinion!

A long time ago, I considered this viewpoint, and concluded that I did not have enough knowledge to accept it. As a teenager, I came to the conclusion that such a claim would be both irrational and totally arrogant—irrational, because no one has such knowledge—and arrogant, because to claim such knowledge is impossible. What appealed to me far more was the agnostic view,[1] which was certainly not so easily shown to be irrational, and which also had some humility suited to the limited intellect of human beings.

Agnosticism was the view popularized by Darwin's friend, T. H. Huxley, who also viewed atheism in the way I did. What I find quite amazing about the present time is that there are actually people in the world who

1. "I do not know if there is a god."

claim to be atheists. How did they come to this belief, this faith-system? That is the only way it can be described, since no atheist I have encountered has yet claimed to have total knowledge of absolutely everything, a claim which would easily be open to testing!

Judging from the strength of some atheist opinions, they presumably have access to a secret source of information known only to themselves. There are atheists who have stated openly on the internet that since *they* consider Christians to be irrational, they can only envisage violence as the way of helping Christians to see what they call reason! And of course, as Peter Hitchens, the Christian brother of the late atheist Christopher Hitchens, demonstrated so clearly in a recent book,[2] Marxist atheists tried state-inspired violence against Christianity, and the result was that Christianity grew. Of course, there is an ancient Chinese proverb which states that the person who resorts to violence admits thereby that he has lost the argument!

But what calls forth this intemperate outburst from these atheists? Have they perhaps heard a voice calling out from the sky, "It's all right—God really doesn't exist!"? Mysticism is perhaps the only way in which an atheist can cling to his opinion whilst believing he is also rational. And atheists will never convince the ordinary rational Christian this way.

If Christianity is true, it is not surprising that venomous attacks have been made against it from every conceivable angle. The Christian view of humankind is that we are in rebellion against our creator and in desperate need, instead of being masters of our fate. Science today clearly points to our ultimate total extermination by the forces of the universe around us, unless an alternative possibility such as Christianity is true. Because of this, the only possible secular basis for morality is human preferences, which rarely agree! Into this hopeless situation, the evidence-based religion of Christ brings hope, meaning and a morality based on love.

Sampling an atheist opinion in philosophy

Let us look at one or two specimen atheists. By this I do not mean the high profile "new atheists," such as Richard Dawkins and Christopher Hitchens, whose views have been validly criticized by writers such as Alister McGrath, Peter Hitchens and others, including more serious atheist thinkers such as Michael Ruse.[3] I mean those atheists who try to follow a common-sense route of thinking.

2. Hitchens, *Rage*.
3. Ruse, "Dawkins disrepute."

For instance, we might look at the philosopher Julian Baggini, who has committed his basic opinions to print.[4] I had hoped before reading this book that he would first deal with the problem of no evidence for the atheist position, but it was not to be. For instance, in his first chapter, he stated, "My main aim in this book is to provide a positive case for atheism, one that is not simply about rubbishing religious belief. In other words, I hope it will be as much about why one should be an atheist, as why one should *not* be a theist." I read on in hope, but three pages on, I encountered a comment on evangelical Christians in relation to those car bumper stickers which ask you to honk if you love Jesus. Baggini stated, "The crass simplicity of this world view can be darkly comic, in that it throws into relief how easy it is for humans to give in to comforting idiocy."

It so happens that I can be described as an evangelical Christian, a worldview I eventually came to hold long after rejecting atheism as irrational and approaching the matter of religious faith as an open-minded agnostic. It is important for agnostics to have open minds, for otherwise they betray their belief that they have not been able to make up their mind one way or another. But if they *do* make up their minds, they stop being agnostics! What struck me was not simply that Dr Baggini made this particular criticism of my worldview, because I have encountered far worse (!), but that he had not laid any foundation for his assertions. I think this shows a little of his bias!

When he moved on to considering evidence for and against atheism, Baggini asserted, "all the strong evidence tells in favor of atheism, and only weak evidence tells against it." In fact, he seemed so certain of this that he repeated it almost in the same words only one page later. When he came to consider what he called weak evidence, he then set up an Aunt Sally of evidence for life after death, and knocked it down to his satisfaction. When Baggini considered strong evidence, he wrote of natural law and seemed to think this was in atheism's favor, without considering that many Christians with experience of research science (like myself) fully accept natural law. Indeed it is only because of this acceptance that Christians can talk of the miraculous, a matter which I discuss in a subsequent chapter. And as a scientist, I am not so dogmatic as to exclude the miraculous, because if I do so, I may miss something of the utmost importance.

I think that Baggini's compartmentalization (naturalism versus supernaturalism) is really another form of bias in his thinking! I would love to discuss what I have written subsequently in this book with him. Even if he does not accept my argument, he may (perhaps, one hopes) revise his

4. Baggini, *Atheism*.

opinion of evangelical Christians! I think his biggest problem comes when he considers morals, and arrives only at the criterion of human preferences for these important matters (well, perhaps not all such preferences—he appears selective, or as I would say, biased). The reader will have to read the rest of my book to see why human moral and ethical preference is a problem, and what the Christian answer is.

Bias in the study of history

Dr Baggini is a philosopher, and I consider philosophy an important subject for Christians. For my other example of atheist bias, I would like to include history, also a very important subject for Christians, so let us move on to a historian who claims to be an atheist, Robin Lane Fox.[5] His book purports to deal with the Bible as a historical work. What intrigued me when I read it was the statement in his acknowledgements, "... my views of the early history of the Hebrew Scriptures have been formed by the insights of J. Wellhausen, more than a century ago. Modern attempts to depart from their main principles have mostly confirmed me in the widely shared acceptance that Wellhausen was right." Perhaps he did not know that Wellhausen was an anti-Semitic German nationalist who took a "Hegelian" view of factual data. (On being told that his theory of history conflicted with the known facts, the philosopher Hegel once said, "So much the worse for the facts!") Wellhausen was arrogant and totally dismissive of evidence which proved him wrong. His views on the origin of the Old Testament, or Hebrew Bible, are unsubstantiated by archaeology, and largely without any evidence of any sort. I have a book, *Lex Mosaica*, published in 1894 by a panel of distinguished scholars including linguists and archaeologists, which takes him and other so-called "higher critics" to task for their very arrogant views. The clear evidence of archaeology never seems to have played any part in forming the opinions of these critics!

Understanding Wellhausen—a game

To try to understand Wellhausen, let us have a little game. In 2011, for the very first time, I went to Normandy and saw the famous Bayeux Tapestry. Let us be clear what this tapestry really is.[6] European historians and

5. Fox, *The Unauthorized Version*.
6. Wilson, *Bayeux Tapestry*, 12-13.

archaeologists virtually unite on the following details. The tapestry is not a tapestry, but a superb embroidery produced soon after the Norman invasion of England in 1066 AD. It was probably a gift for Bishop Odo of Bayeux, a half-brother of William the Conqueror, and was made in the south of England before 1082. It was mentioned in the inventory of Bayeux Cathedral in 1476, and engravings of it were published in two volumes of a famous French book in 1729-30. It was nearly ruined during the French Revolution, on at least two occasions, but in 1803, Napoleon had it exhibited in a museum in Paris as propaganda for his proposed invasion of England ("We beat the English once and we can do it again.") which never happened!

Now, let us imagine we are extreme English nationalists, and do not like the French. (I actually think they are wonderful people, who have given the world some excellent wines and food!) What do we do about the Norman Conquest, in relation to the Bayeux Tapestry's account of the French beating the English? Well, for a start, we can say that it was forged by the French for Napoleon's exhibition in 1803, and the Norman Conquest never really happened. But what about the references to the tapestry in the fifteenth century? Well, we can write them off as not relating to *this* tapestry! And what about the engravings of it in the eighteenth century? Well, they were later forgeries to give credibility to the tapestry!

This is the same cavalier approach to science, archaeology and history adopted by Professor Julius Wellhausen. He clearly did not like Judaism, and wanted to show that early Jewish history was not as the Old Testament (the Hebrew Bible) recorded it. He took a tentative idea of a few earlier scholars, that there were several separate and conflicting documents which had been poorly edited together by several editors to produce the early history of Israel, and built upon it his own fantasy that very little in the Old Testament came from before the seventh century BC. The accuracy of his opinions may be judged by the simple fact that the book of Deuteronomy, which he dated to the seventh century BC, has been shown clearly, by archaeological data, to have a structure corresponding to documents of the fourteenth and thirteenth centuries BC, and certainly not six hundred years later! (Obviously forgery by some schemers!) But the most telling argument against Wellhausen is that absolutely no evidence has been found to corroborate his amazing fantasies! A great deal of evidence has been found *against* them, however, and an enormous amount of evidence corroborates the reliability of the biblical documents as we have them.[7] It is amazing that

---

7. Kitchen, *Reliability*.

anyone still clings to Wellhausen's discredited nonsense, but there seem to be hopeful atheists everywhere! (So much the worse for the facts!)

Robin Lane Fox and the New Testament

With Mr. Fox's acknowledgment to Wellhausen, my appetite was whetted! Sure enough, I did not have long to wait. Mr. Fox started querying the writing of Luke, the early gentile (non-Jewish) Christian who wrote a Gospel and the book of the Acts of the Apostles. According to Fox, Luke was apparently wrong about a number of historical statements in his Gospel, particularly concerning the events surrounding the birth of Jesus. The matters to which Mr. Fox refers were all answered very clearly by the late veteran Christian scholar Professor F.F. Bruce in a book first published in 1943.[8] The last (sixth) edition was published in 1981. Nowhere in Mr. Fox's book does he appear to refer to this eminent scholar, so I can only assume that he has not read him. Bruce pointed out Luke's amazing historical accuracy in all matters, such as the precise titles accorded to Roman officials, and gave a clear refutation of Fox's opinions long before they were first published in 1991. I ask myself as a Christian who takes a serious view of research scholarship and history, why should I take any notice of Fox's questionable opinions? He is perhaps one who agrees with Hegel, "So much the worse for the facts!"

The sad bias problems of so-called "liberal" Christianity

Until recently, I thought that all those who considered themselves under this heading had accepted the "higher criticism" views of the Bible simply because they thought this accorded more with their interpretation of the human faculty of reason. They have historically tended to put human reason above the authority of the written words of the Bible. I sympathize with their high view of reason, and I too have a high view of reason, but I think that they may have done violence to the way God communicates with us. Their views have led some of them to deny the deity of Christ, and of the Holy Spirit, and obviously the Holy Trinity also, which I consider to be the totally unique view of God revealed in the Bible, and the absolutely essential center of the Christian faith. However, recently I have encountered

---

8. Bruce, *New Testament Documents*.

some evidence which sheds a more worrying light on the origins of liberalism in Christianity.

The anti-Semitic views of scholars like Wellhausen were apparently endemic in some aspects of biblical criticism from the nineteenth century onwards.[9] It is difficult not to see this as the real motivation of some German critical scholars. The recent publication of a book widely acclaimed by scholars, dealing with the extremes of biblical criticism and anti-Semitism under the Hitler regime, is even more worrying.[10] The German Christian movement, apparently responding to comments like that of the Nazi Alfred Rosenberg's that Jesus was Jewish, invented a Jesus from Galilee, who was supposedly not Jewish, and who was persecuted and finally crucified by the Jews. Leading scholars like Gerhard Kittel openly supported anti-Semitism, and even the noted Old Testament scholar, Gerhard von Rad, though politically moving away from the Nazis to the Confessing Church movement which opposed the German Christian movement, signed his letters "Heil Hitler" to the end of the Nazi era.

The peak achievement of the German Christian movement was marked by publication of a de-Judaized bible called the "Message of God". The entire Old Testament was omitted, the four Gospels were re-written as one narrative, and large sections of the New Testament written by the obviously Jewish writers Matthew and Paul were also left out. Such violence to the scriptures of Christianity is breath-taking!

The abandonment of biblical authority by biased liberal Christians has led to yet further damaging events in our own time. The adoption of openly un-biblical behavior in some churches in the United States includes persecution of Christians who cannot accept these deviations.[11] Leaders of congregations who have tried to leave what they saw as rank apostasy have been subjected to vexatious and expensive civil lawsuits by manipulative authorities, despite St Paul's severe comments on such behavior in 1 Cor 6.[12,13,14] Indeed, manipulation is the only "ethic" acceptable to people who have openly espoused postmodernism! Even bishops have been ousted for believing the Bible, including a bishop known to me!

9. Hexham, *Understanding World Religions*, 363-6.
10. Heschel, *Aryan Jesus*.
11. Anglican Curmudgeon, "*Episcopal Church.*"
12. Wikipedia, "*Dennis Canon.*"
13. Anglican Curmudgeon, "*Dennis Canon loses.*"
14. Ashworth, "Briefing Paper."

The only comment that I can offer is that some theological liberals, worshiping the false god of postmodernism in the name of tolerance, have become the most intolerant people in the entire Christian Church.

Secular intolerance of Christians

However, lest anyone be led to believe that theological liberals are the only people who are intolerant of Bible-believing Christians, a book by the former Archbishop of Canterbury, Lord Carey, and his journalist son, Andrew, has placed on record some of the secular attacks on Christians in the UK.[15]

The frankly idiotic extremes of postmodernism would be something to laugh at, if they did not lead to real harassment of ordinary Christians who simply try to live a Christian life in a world which is increasingly anti-Christian. As the Careys point out, there are even high court judges in the UK who appear to be totally ignorant of the Christian faith, its history in the UK, and its normal practice. For instance, one senior judge even considered that Christianity was irrelevant to modern justice, dismissing it with remarks that "bordered on the contemptuous," and thereby compelled a good Christian man to leave a job he had done well. This judge's views receive extended attention in the Careys' book. To me, the judge's opinions on Christianity are as ludicrous as the ancient Roman belief that the first Christians were atheists, because they refused to acknowledge Caesar as Lord!

A specimen of bias in evangelical and reformed Christians

Well, now that I have mentioned a couple of atheists, some liberal Christians, and UK secularism, readers may be wondering whether I think all evangelical and reformed Christians are squeaky-clean, totally unbiased(!) paragons of virtue! The answer, of course, is that I do not. Some Christians, for instance, take a remarkably aggressive stance, not only against the world in general, but also against many other Christians, over the matter of biological evolution.

Let us be clear what the concept of evolution explains. It explains the vast arrays of fossils found on the earth, the reason why earlier ones appear much simpler than more recent ones, why certain radioactive elements are

---

15. Carey and Carey, *We Don't do God*.

commoner in some layers of rock than others, and why, for instance, human remains are not found in the same layers of rock as dinosaurs. The apparent footprints of human beings in the Paluxy river bed, Texas, alongside genuine footprints of dinosaurs, were shown by 1980 to be carvings dating from within the last millennium.[16] Evolution also explains why some living creatures have become extinct, and why some have dominated their habitats. It also explains the overall development of many different types of creature and plant in terms of chemistry, biochemistry, and embryology.

What evolution does not explain is also clear. It does not explain why there is anything at all, nor does it explain why any universe (if there are other universes) should have such amazing complexity as we find in ours, or why certain physical constants exist at levels which precisely allow this complexity.[17] As a development theory, it has much to commend it. Without it, we could not understand the earth as it is. But as to purpose, or meaning, or ethics, it shows us nothing apart from the brute forces of circumstance. In short, evolution is about history.

There is a historical reason why some Christians are so vehement in denouncing evolution. This is that certain atheists seem to think evolution is some sort of argument against the truth of the Bible. These Christians, without thinking that the atheists might be mistaken (why not?), actually accepted the atheist arguments and thought they had to oppose evolution.

Denis Alexander has written an excellent account of the historical development of modern "fiat" creationism.[18] The Latin word "fiat" means "let it be done" and these Christians decided that the biblical account of creation was meant to rule out evolution as though it were a competing theory. Other Christians, like myself, take the view that the Bible deals with the *origin* of the universe in its account of creation by God. History, including evolution, is another matter. I will say more about this later.

I went through a "fiat" creationist phase myself!

About three years after becoming a Christian, I became a "fiat" creationist for a while. I had read some of the arguments from this point of view, and tended at first to accept them. But as I make clear later, it seemed to me to require a false interpretation of the Bible at some points. When I also

16. Berry, *God and Evolution*, 122–4.
17. Rees, *Just Six Numbers*.
18. Alexander, *Rebuilding the Matrix*, 289–329.

found it required the compression of very long periods of time, and the acceptance of very dubious ideas about science, and when I came across some of the other ideas which I state in this present book, I concluded that it was not true. Later I encountered some very pointed polemics. Indeed, Denis Alexander quotes one of these "fiat" creationists, Henry Morris (whose book *The Genesis Flood*,[19] written with John Whitcomb, I read soon after becoming a Christian in 1960), writing in 1980 that, ". . . it is possible to be a Christian and an evolutionist. Likewise, one can be a Christian thief, or a Christian adulterer, or a Christian liar!" I do not understand why he was so uncharitable, but then I would hesitate to use such comparisons against "fiat" creationists. They are simply misguided, not immoral.

Nor do I understand why any Christians accept the illogical atheist argument that evolution (a historical matter) necessarily rules out creation (a matter of ultimate origins). After all, atheists accept the irrational belief that there is no god (which implies they know everything about the universe as well as what is outside it). Perhaps Christians need to learn that some other atheist beliefs are irrational as well, instead of accepting the bias of atheist arguments!

But there is one very big further consideration which weighs with me today. When I talk about Christianity with atheists or agnostics, they frequently bring up this question. I wonder what they think about the strong polemics against science in which some Christians indulge. As many Christians are not "fiat" creationists, perhaps it would be better if the latter were to state that being a Christian (and therefore believing in creation) does *not* mean you have to alter your views about evolution. There are also one or two matters which I have mentioned later in chapter 20, where Biblical truth seems to require a different view from that of the "fiat" creationists.

So for the moment, let us note that Christians may exhibit bias. They may exhibit a variety of biases, but perhaps we should draw a line between those biases which are essential to Christian belief (such as the open mind which does not rule out miracles *a priori*), and those which, like "fiat" creationism are not essential to a belief in the good news about Jesus. One of my views about evolution is that it could *only* have occurred through the work of an amazing creator! The probabilities of it happening in the only universe we know are otherwise unbelievable.

---

19. Whitcomb and Morris, *Genesis Flood*.

Why bias matters

Many people think it is possible to approach life in a neutral way. The problem is that there is no evidence for this common belief. All people have different core beliefs which undergird their approach to science and morals, and neutrality is an illusion. However, perhaps there is a way for all people to approach real life on a common basis, and that is the subject of this little book. This approach depends on starting with the simplest aspects of human experience. What is the bias in such an approach?

First, it means you need to be open to anything. Nothing can be ruled out *a priori*. Secondly, it means you need to be willing to use your mind, and not simply accept what other people say. Clearly you may build your opinion on the basis of what you consider well-established facts, but if you should come to find that these "facts" are not only questionable but downright false, then perhaps you should adjust your opinion accordingly. I have done this several times in my life.

So what is my bias?

I have a bias, and it is to follow where the evidence apparently leads, examining it critically, and reforming my opinions as best I may. I do not rule out the apparently impossible on rationalist grounds as do those who dogmatically espouse atheism and some other religions, though I will certainly use reason as a tool. I try to start with the most basic experiences which I think we share, although I could be wrong in my opinion on this matter. I do not claim that I have full knowledge of the whole universe and outside it, as atheists do implicitly. If you want to follow the reasoning and experience which has brought me to firm belief in the very special God of Christianity, then this book is an attempt to make the argument clear. How do I think the argument goes?

First, we all seem to experience something. I try to categorize some of the simplest elements of that something. From these elements, I move to the thought that we have questions posed to us by our experience. From what scientific investigation has reasonably established, I conclude that all human existence will have to end eventually in the future, and that science has never produced any reason for moral or ethical behavior. The only scientific reason for any moral code is that human beings have preferences. Unfortunately, human beings differ widely on what is good and bad! This ultimately gives us a choice between a police state (but who makes the rules?) and anarchy (everyone fighting for their own preferences). However, we could consider not the ending of all human existence, but its origin (why do *persons* exist?) and the origin of the whole universe (*not* its history, as from the big bang or what preceded it but why it actually came to exist).

The question of origins leads us into the fact that human beings manifest personality, and most other things do not. So is the ultimate origin of everything personal or impersonal? If it is *impersonal*, then again we are stuck with the problem of what is good and bad. In an impersonal universe, anything goes: so if we want law, it's the police state; if we don't like law, then we muddle along fighting as we go. Some atheist police states have been amazingly violent. I think the outstanding example of an atheist ethic derived from biological science (survival of the fittest) is that of China under Chairman Mao. He managed to kill over seventy million people in peacetime, nearly forty million of them in the "Great Leap Forward."[20]

It is no accident that police states have originated largely in communist, fascist and Islamic countries. Real democracy appears to emerge usually against a Christian background, although democracy is not without its problems. Mohammed believed in a God who is a person, but I have met intellectual Muslims who think of him more as a force, and the very term "Islam" means "submission."

But if the origin of everything is *personal*, then we have other options. If the universe *itself* is a personal entity, then we are again stuck, because in it there are things considered good or bad by all people; which are good things, and which are bad things again depend on the person making the decision, and of course people differ on this matter!

However, if there is a *person* who originated or created the universe, then there may be a way out of the maze of human disagreements. How can we know about such an origin? Only by the person letting us know. It may be surprising, but if you ignore the numerous unsubstantiated claims by cultists to have a special revelation from God over the last century and a half, there are only three historical claims worth considering. These are Judaism, Christianity and Islam. Out of these, I arrive at Christianity for numerous reasons, many of which will become apparent. Like a huge number of people both past and present, what the universe seems to me to demand is the very special God of Christianity, a God I call a *super-person* because he is three persons in one God.

Now, if you wish, sit back and read on . . .

20. Chang and Halliday, *Mao*.

2

Why it matters what we believe

Simply in order to live, we have answered certain questions by implication, consciously or unconsciously

DOES IT MATTER HOW you live? Can't you just muddle along and trust to luck? Why bother about the many ridiculous and conflicting religions and philosophies which human beings have dreamed up? *"Tell me one good reason why I should show even the slightest concern about what I believe."*

Here is one good reason: if you don't bother, you may get hurt. People who live inconsistently or muddle along may do things which endanger themselves. For a bet, an American put four bullets in a revolver, spun the chamber and shot himself dead.[1] He didn't bother about elementary mathematics. He ignored the simple probability that two chances in six is less than four in six. He was more likely to die, and he did.

"But I wouldn't do anything as daft as that."

Here is another good reason: someone or something else may hurt you. We know that great white sharks don't want to eat human beings. If they bite a bit off, they don't usually come back for more. But the shark has poor eyesight. If you swim on the surface of the ocean when a great white's about, it looks up and thinks, "Great! another stupid seal!" Its eyesight is so poor that it will even attack an empty surf-board. But it stops there. Surf-board is not on the menu.

You may get hurt... something may hurt you... you may hurt someone else. Yes, I have plenty of opportunities for that. But why should it matter to me? Well, hurt someone you don't like, and maybe you get hurt back. Hurt someone you *do* like, and you may hurt as a result.

1. Darwin Awards, *"More Candidates,"* para. 3.

But isn't it all a bit of a game?

Some people play with religions and philosophies the way other people play computer games. It isn't real, so have a bit of fun. If you get eaten by a dragon in the dungeon, real life goes on anyway. But have you thought of this? Even fantasy is a part of reality. Playing games is part of life, from the idiot who gambles with his and other people's lives on the roads, to children playing hopscotch in the playground. They both seem real at the time, but the real point is that they are tests: can I achieve this? Can I make sixty before the next traffic light? Can I reach the end of the hopscotch without putting a foot wrong? Games are ways in which we test our ability in an atmosphere we find congenial. Games give us a sense of achievement, of beating the computer, or perhaps other drivers, or other children. There is even evidence that intellectual games may help you avoid dementia in old age. I love my Sudoku!

So playing with religion and philosophy becomes an intellectual game; you want to prove that you are better than some poor nincompoop who goes to church, or who believes that the universe is a living organism. Well, yes, that may be the aim of some. But if you want to show that all religion or philosophy is wrong, there is a problem. The problem is that *everyone* has a religion or philosophy of life. *"Pardon?"* Yes, even the most thorough-going skeptic has to live. And perhaps those unhappy people who take their own lives do so because of what they believe.

Everyone has a religion or philosophy of life

Yes, everyone. Some people call it a religion, although the line dividing religion and philosophy is not clear. Philosophy and religion deal with similar concerns. A philosophy is a system of thought, and human beings are thinking animals. Somewhere, even in the most disordered person's mind, there are a few thoughts which link with reality. These thoughts also constitute part of reality. Let's keep it quite simple. In fact it *is* quite simple. There are only three basic aspects to the reality we experience: what am I? what is true? and what shall I do? The whole of life revolves around these questions. Even if they are not *consciously* asked, the answers to them underlie all human behavior.

What am I?

This is a central question about values, meaning and identity. There is something about *me* that is different from everything else. We use words like personality and identity to describe that special aspect of *me*-ness which can only be understood from within. What is my identity? And what is meant by personality, a concept which differs from a thing?

At this point we are forced to consider our basic experience. The distinction between *me* and *everything else* is clear to me, but for another person, whose experience I can never know first-hand, what I consider *me* is part of his or her *everything else*.

This is perhaps the most basic aspect of personality—the distinction between subject and object, between me and everything else. It is also the foundation of identity—a unique status which, for instance, may be described as the occupation of a particular part of space and time.

The answer to the question "What am I?" is fundamental to everything we think and do. If we can give a reasonable account of it, we shall include an understanding of the whole of our experience, of the reality outside us as well as within us.

What is true?

There are certain obvious truths in our experience. One is that we had a beginning. We did not always exist. This is a limit. We may learn of things which happened before we were born, but only through intermediaries: we did not *experience* these events or matters.

The experience of a beginning leads on to another matter: there is *sequence*. Events in this space-time universe have an arrangement: they occur at different times and places. We even may infer causality from some of them; that is, we say one event comes before a second event, and that the second event would not have occurred without the first one. This shows us another truth of experience: there is order, of a sort.

A further truth is that we have other limits. We may be exposed to them in obvious ways, as when we reach the limit of intellectual or physical endeavor in some task. There may be some limits which we shall experience only once in a lifetime, such as death.

All these subjects need further examination, but for now we shall continue our survey of what matters, and why.

What shall I do?

Every action we perform relates either to what we need or desire for ourselves, or to what we perceive as our obligations to other people or things. In every action, therefore, there is an implied answer to the two previous questions. For instance, when we eat food, one implication may be that our physical construction requires a physical input of energy to maintain its function. Another may be that we like and desire the specific food and see it as a source of enjoyment. Or perhaps we may be preparing ourselves to work for someone else. These implications relate to our understanding of what is true, and how we see ourselves.

Of course, our actions may be inconsistent. Many people who smoke tobacco do so to satisfy a desire which has unfortunately become an addiction, yet they would dearly like to quit the habit. In this case, the addiction has proved more powerful than they are, and needs treatment if they are to beat it.

On the other hand, our actions may be consistent with our answers to the first two questions, but unfortunately we have the wrong answers. There is nothing which makes one human race inherently better than another, yet some people act as though this is true. And all too frequently one person wrongly implies that there is a degraded motive for the actions of another: this may arise when a person of one race is given a job in preference to someone of another race; it is all too easy to label the decision racially biased, whatever the real reasons for it.

From this, it will be seen that motives are often difficult to fathom, and may be at the root of many discords in life. Nevertheless, our actions will arise from what we believe, even if our beliefs are not easy to uncover. Let us put to rest the pretence of some atheists that they "do not have beliefs or faith." A belief is something you consider to be true, either self-evidently, or on the ground of some argument. And a faith is trusting in a belief or a system of beliefs. We all have a faith in something, and as we saw, faith that there is no god is just about the most irrational faith you can have! Without complete knowledge of what is true, you cannot know this.

On the other hand, you do not need complete knowledge of everything to be a Christian, but enough to convince you. The question is, what is the evidence? As I state in later chapters, the nature of the universe is important. So is the question of *origins*, not merely of *history*, and within the question of origins there is a huge question about the personality of individual people. If life is a result of chance events, then why are there billions of accumulations of highly organized groups of molecules on earth, each one *thinking of himself or herself as a distinct person*?! How can an accidental or chance event result in even one single small chunk of reality *thinking* of itself as a person?

Discord and inconsistency

These three questions—what am I? what is true? and what shall I do?—are of considerable significance in our lives, as the answers we give to them may affect both our perceptions and behavior. For instance, if I answer them in part by saying that my race is of considerable importance and that people of some other races are not important, I may conclude that it does not matter how I behave towards such people. Because some people have given such answers, we have the many problems of racism today. This is a source of human discord and pain.

Another source of problems is when we give incompatible answers to the three questions. If it is true, for example, that human beings are merely thinking animals, then there is little point in saying that we should obey laws, which are simply conventions produced by other thinking animals. The idea that laws are breakable if you can get away with it is a recipe for more pain. Indeed, there is some inconsistency in trying to bring pressure on others by breaking the laws. If you want the law to be changed, what kind of a message is it to break it? The behavior of groups of activists in breaking the law carries its own message, one which their followers may not always realize. The message is quite different from the one which they are actually trying to convey. Instead of saying, "This matter is so terrible that we feel we actually must break the law," their actions may convey to others the message, "Law does not matter, and it is easy to break, so anyone can do what they like."

Unfortunately, the idea of anarchy has caught on quite widely in today's world. There is a common thread of thought running through some unelected pressure groups, from animal rights supporters to terrorists, to the effect that there is no limit on what may be done to further "the cause." Breaking the law, sometimes in a way which seems sick or sadistic, suggests to others that these terrorists are largely psychopaths who should be resisted with all the powers society can muster against them.

The importance of law

Law matters to all of us, as it is for the regulation of human behavior in its more extreme forms. We need protection and consistency in our lives. In addition to all the provisions of criminal law, there is also the civil law which can bring people to account for their actions. Accountability is essential to life. If there were no laws, people who were hurt, or their relatives, might respond with equally savage or even more savage acts. Lawlessness brings destruction and misery.

Consequently, we may appreciate that the answers to basic questions matter hugely to human society. At the level of the individual human being, the history of nations is determined. What we human beings believe, and how we act in consequence, are matters which should concern us all. In the next chapter, we shall look at how we may *start* to examine our beliefs and actions.

3

Where do I begin?

What are the simplest aspects of our experience?

OVER FIFTY YEARS AGO, I was discussing matters of basic belief with a friend at my university who had very different perspectives from mine. He said something which has always stuck with me: "I can only start with myself. That's all I have."

At first sight, some might laugh. How ridiculous! What about the world, and indeed the universe in all its complexity and variety? But in one sense, he was right. How do you know anything about that world? How do you begin? Indeed, is there anything outside the dream I'm dreaming? How can you demonstrate objectivity, namely, that there is a reality distinct from your imagination? These are hard questions, particularly in the modern world with its psychoanalytical theories: they may postulate hidden depths to your imagination and conflicting aspects within your personality.

One problem is that even to talk about these matters, we have to take many things for granted. Language, for instance: where did it come from? A huge variety of experiences which make up our lives to now: what are they, and do they have any meaning at all?

Some of us will be scared of what has been called the void: is there ultimately anything? What are our lives about? Perhaps we should not enquire too deeply, in case we find something which worries us to the point of derangement. One of history's great thinkers, the skeptic David Hume, ended his discourse on human understanding with a cry from his heart: "Where am I, or what?"[1] He then intimated that this question had no an-

---

1. Hume, *Treatise of Human Nature*, 316.

swer and the best we could do was to go and forget it by having a game with some friends.

Beginning with naïve experience

It is always best to begin any enterprise by taking stock of where you are and how matters have developed to date. If you wish to make a beginning, one simple way is to list your experiences and see where they lead. If this is the absolute beginning, then the experience needs to be naïve, which is to say it should be at the most basic level.

This is a point at which human language is inadequate. If we describe something in words, in one sense we have categorized it already. We may sense therefore that there are no established rules for what we are about to embark upon. A beginning is exactly that—nothing comes before it. Consequently, what I am about to do may differ from what you would do in the same situation. Perhaps your beginning is different from mine. I would ask you, however, to consider whether there is enough agreement with your experience for you to see where it all leads, and perhaps to find it a helpful approach.

One other issue is that I have no claim to perfection. Maybe what I am doing is wrong, for reasons totally unknown to me or you. One useful test will be experiment, finding whether it all corresponds with the "reality" you experience. Scientists try to progress from what is known to an understanding of what is presently unknown, and they use two tools: reason and experiment. Neither tool is sufficient on its own, but together they are a powerful force to further our understanding.

What is naïve experience?

What are the very simplest experiences you can imagine? Of course, you have language to express them in, and a wealth of other experiences to build upon. However, if you are to consider where you are now, the best place to start is at the simplest experiences which you can imagine you had as a baby. So, as a baby, what do you think first impressed itself upon you?

The first thing I can think of is a matter to which some very famous people have drawn attention. One of the greatest mathematicians, Gottfried Wilhelm Leibniz (1646–1716) is recorded as asking, "Why is there something rather than nothing?" And a more recent philosopher, Jean-Paul

Where do I begin?

Sartre (1905–1980), said that the fundamental philosophical question was why anything existed.

Something or nothing?

So this is what I consider the starting point. There is something rather than nothing. This is the basic human experience, from which no one can escape. And it is a naïve experience: in terms of our language, nothing can be more basic than saying that we all experience something.

We have to put it that way, because we have not yet tried to deal with the question of what the something is. Is it a dream, entirely within the imagination? Are you at this moment manufacturing me and all I have said so far as a product of your imagination? Of course, most of us tend to assume that there is an objective world outside our imagination, although it may sometimes be hard to draw the line between the two! But for the sake of completeness, we should note that there have been people who have adhered to solipsism.[2]

The solipsist takes the view that the only thing he can know is himself, and this argument is very powerful. Rather than dismiss it out of hand, which is not a rational action, we need to consider it further, and see its implications at a future point in this discourse. But for the moment, because we can take as a fact of experience that most of us are not solipsists, let us go further along the path of naïve experience.

Order or chaos?

The next thing which you may have noticed as a baby, though without defining it, is that the *something* has a structure. There are regularities in experience. Of course, from our vantage point of reflection as mature adults, we may take the view that some of these regularities are the result of our minds imposing an order on the rich variety of our experiences. That is true in part, but there are many ways in which order is discernable in the simplest things we experience.

Take, for instance, my view at this moment. I notice through the window in front of me that some of the objects I see are sticking up out of the ground and there are predominantly green flat shapes of things which I

---

2. Latin: *solus ipse*: self alone

recognize as leaves. Some other green or brown things are more tubular and topped with delicate things in a wide variety of colors: scarlet, blue, yellow, purple, pink, white and cream. These I call stems, trunks and flowers.

Different levels and types of order

As a scientist, I may go much further, and relate these beautiful objects to a variety of processes which are involved in their growth and reproduction, and their interactions with the other objects which I recognize as birds and insects. It is difficult to call my garden a chaos, however much I may neglect it or find it difficult to cultivate. There are many different levels of order within it. The levels themselves constitute a form of order. In one way, they contribute to what we perceive as beauty, although this is a very difficult thing to define. Even where one form of order begins to break down, as with the death of an animal, other forms of order are involved as the biochemical and bacterial decay of the body begins. This is also an ordered process, far from chaos.

Indeed, we have a real problem in trying to imagine chaos at all. For instance, the mathematical concept of variety (for instance, of human heights or weights) is far from chaos: Sir Francis Galton (1822–1911) was amazed at the beauty and symmetry of the bell-shaped "normal distribution," which he described as order reigning in the middle of chaos. Even when things seem to us to be very chaotic, there may be forms of order underlying them which are exact and precise.

That there is order, rather than chaos, is a fundamental assumption or axiom of all science. It is also the basis for virtually all human behavior. Imagine how hopeless it would be if we were unable to assume that our past experiences would be repeated in the future: any activity, no matter how trivial, would become a hair-raising, anxiety-provoking, outlandishly frightening extreme level of experiment! Why should a cookery recipe turn out similarly on two separate occasions? (If you are like me, maybe it doesn't, but I'm talking about people who understand cooking, like my wife.) Why should not a person, who smiled and said, "Hello," to us yesterday, perhaps frown and beat us to a pulp today? Of course we may think such ideas are ludicrous, but that is because we assume order on the basis of our previous experience. If we do not assume order, life is going to be very hard!

Where do I begin?

Unity and diversity

The varieties of order in our naïve experience bring us on to another matter of interest. Overall, our experience has a sort of unity. Furthermore, within our experience, many things may seem linked together, such as leaves, flowers, birds or insects in the garden which I mentioned earlier. There are many levels and groups which show an overall unity, with the members of the group sharing a variety of characteristics; yet within each group there is a diversity which depends on the members showing individual differences.

For instance, plants and animals come in several million different sorts, yet we can usually recognize them as members of these two groups. Furthermore, we class both plants and animals as living organisms, and there are other things (such as viruses) which we may recognize as living, but perhaps have difficulty in placing within either the plant or animal group. Perhaps they require a group of their own, but within the greater group of things which are living.

Classification is basic to all aspects of life, so unity and diversity are very basic features of our human experience. We need to remember, too, that overall there appears a huge, all-inclusive unity which embraces everything we experience, everything we have experienced, and everything we will experience. Within that unity, even of a single person's experience, there is an immeasurable wealth of diversity. And with that thought of past, present and future, we pass on to another feature of naïve experience.

Sequence

Many years ago, when I first thought about these matters, I used the heading "time" to describe this aspect of experience. I realized after a while that "time" was not quite the term I sought. I really wanted to describe more what we experience with the passage of time, not time itself. There is change, and some events lead to other events: these are the two groups of experience which I place under the heading "sequence."

Change is easy enough to recognize. Something moves or alters its color, shape, smell, sound or feel. This happens so frequently that we notice the occasional absence of change as unusual: the solitude of a remote coast for the city-dweller, for instance, or the absence of the gradual progress of the day for someone working in an air-conditioned, brightly-lit office-block with the venetian blinds closed for a few hours.

God's Fingerprints

Causation is more than change

Events leading to other events may be more or less than they seem. I remember a statistics professor telling me years ago that in the parts of Amsterdam where there are more storks, more babies are also born. Now in English mythology, a stork carries the baby to its parents. (Of course, the English are not completely stupid; they do know the truth about where babies come from, but when a child is too young to understand, or when the parents are too tired to explain, some people tell this story.)

The professor in question then explained that it was not the storks which caused the babies (are you surprised?), but that the babies perhaps caused the storks in an indirect manner. Where there were more families, they needed more houses, so the babies in a sense "caused" this. Where there were more Dutch houses, there were more gable roofs, and since the storks looked for roofs of this sort to build their nests, the causal chain ran in a different direction. This is an important story; the moral is that two things may be connected (associated) but not necessarily related as cause and effect. Indeed, since it takes time to build a house, and time for a couple to set up home in one, perhaps we could say that the houses "caused" both the babies and storks.

Self and non-self

The naïve aspects which we have considered will cover much of our experience. There is still one feature which needs attention, though, and it impinges on the matter of solipsism which was mentioned above. This is the distinction most of us draw between what we view as our "self," and everything else which is "outside."

It is a little early to discuss what we mean by the "self," and we shall do that later, but the distinction between "self" and "non-self" is an aspect of the naïve experience of all except solipsists. (Indeed, I would argue that it is an aspect of their experience also, though they do not recognize it, but now is not the time for this. The solipsist's greatest problems come when matters like limitations, origins and destinies are considered, and we shall look further at them then.)

Most people think of the self as something resident in, or identical with, the physical bodies they inhabit. They see themselves as organisms which interact with other similar organisms and many, many objects outside themselves. For them, naïve experience consists of the features we have considered above, but with the additional aspect of a division between themselves and all that is outside.

Bringing it together

So where have we arrived? I like little lists and diagrams to help me think. Here is a list of what we may perceive in our immediate naïve experience. It is a very basic list indeed. For instance, recently I saw a program on television about people who are both deaf and blind. It occurred to me that they might well experience everything I have listed, mainly through sensations such as touch and smell.

NAÏVE EXPERIENCE
something (or nothing)
order (or chaos)
unity and diversity
sequence
self and non-self

Why the opposites?

You may ask why I have included "nothing" and "chaos" in brackets. After all, I have gone to some lengths to say that they are foreign to our experience. The reason is that we may experience an absence of something we normally take for granted, or a marked disorder in something which we feel should be ordered. If a person is so unfortunate as to lose the sense of sight or of hearing, then this may be a profound experience of nothingness in one aspect of naïve experience. The memory may persist and lead to a deep sense of loss, in effect, bereavement. This serves to emphasize that there is indeed something.

Similarly, we may experience apparent disorder which angers or upsets us when, for instance, some group of terrorists perpetrates an outrage. The disorder here is probably in their minds, since they rely on an ordered but relatively free society in which to create their moments of "chaos." They therefore attack the foundation for their own cause, unless it is the cause of chaos. Furthermore, by their actions they imply that no normal person could be expected to agree with their views. Why, indeed, should anyone agree with a demonstrably disordered mind? But again, the apparent disorder these people cause is yet another reminder that order is present, and overwhelmingly powerful.

Dimensions of naïve experience

We may describe these five items as dimensions of naïve experience. There may be other dimensions, but these seem very obvious and therefore a good starting point. Even a child may appreciate them if they are described in simple terms. The next matter to consider is one which most children take for granted, but which adults often do not. Fundamental to almost anything we may do is the matter of trust. What is trustworthy?

4

What can I trust?

Trust and its relationship to our values

OVER THE PAST THIRTY-TWO years in my present church I have known four men who have been married to loving and faithful wives, with pleasant children, and then have walked out to live with another woman.

To me, this seems one of the worst possible betrayals of trust. What is trust? It is depending on someone or something. You depend on a chair to hold you up and not collapse underneath you, and you depend on a person to do certain things for you. When two people have promised solemnly that they will faithfully support each other for life, it is clearly a major let-down if one walks out.

Trust and commitment

The other side of trusting a person is commitment by that person. This is the central aspect of any marriage which works. "For better, for worse, for richer, for poorer, in sickness and in health, till death us do part," as the Church of England prayer book states it. Underlying the commitment is a real, self-giving love of husband and wife to each other.

But not all human betrayal of trust occurs in marriage. It may occur in all kinds of relationships, from employer and employee, to voter and politician. It may occur when a child is abused by an adult, when a quack deceives a needy person who is ill, when a rich employer plunders a pension plan, when a tobacco apologist says that smoking is harmless, or when a surgeon performs a risky operation without fully informing the patient or without appropriate skills.

Trust is about control

Faced with the unreliability of human beings, some turn to other methods of support. Some of a scientific bent put their trust in "facts," while others may seek ways of curbing human behavior by legislation or audit. Yet others may seek hidden (occult) methods of acquiring control over life. The common aim is to have control over events, to make life more predictable.

Whilst trust does not give control, it is in one sense a control. If we can be certain that our trust will be rewarded by a predictable future, we may feel more secure. Hence the feelings of outrage if we are let down: we allowed another person to make us unhappy by giving them the freedom to do so. They infringed our rights; they did not accept their obligations.

Rights and obligations

It is worth looking at this matter of rights and obligations in more depth. Rights are a concept born of law, with penalties to deal with their infringements. There is a compulsion upon people to maintain the rights of others which depends upon the strength of the law. If the law cannot be enforced, it is useless; if the right-abuser feels able to avoid the consequences, the law is powerless to prevent the abuse, whatever the subsequent events.

In contrast, obligations are born of commitment. They are deep within a person's being, something which they would not under any circumstance reject. They have a power to prevent the abuse of another's rights which the law does not. The comedian's statement, "Today I stopped a beautiful girl from being savagely attacked—I controlled myself," takes on a different sense if we can learn that it speaks of obligation rather than rights.

Enlightenment or hypocrisy?

The Enlightenment philosopher, Jean-Jacques Rousseau, was for many people a deeply perplexing man. It was not that he did not believe in rights, but rather that he failed to accept the obligations which his writing implied. For instance, he wrote a book called *Émile, or On Education*, about how a child ideally should be brought up. So what did he do with his five illegitimate children? He put them in an orphanage.[1]

The problem is not that people have no rights; time and again declarations are made to the contrary. The problem is that rights are ignored by others who reject their obligations. It is because of a lack of obligation that some men attack women; the law is powerless to prevent this, although it may possibly deter some. Deterrence is a weak way of attempting to control human behavior.

How then, can obligations be enforced? This is like asking how we can prevent crime. But it takes us to the root of the matter: if obligations could be enforced, laws would be the way. However, the key to performing our obligations lies in the conscience of each one of us. What is conscience? A moral sense of right and wrong. And who decides what is right or wrong?

Right and wrong

At this point in the discussion, you may feel that we are getting way out of our depth. How did we come to this, anyway? We were talking about trust and commitment and now we are considering the deepest problems which afflict mankind. But trust is about behavior, and so is morality. Do you really not care whether someone you trust is right or wrong? Well, perhaps you don't, but this puts you on the same ground as the Marquis de Sade. His view was that things are right because they exist.

But if that is so, then right and wrong don't matter. Surely there are other ways of deciding them? Yes, indeed there are. Countries have constitutions which define what is right. Does this give us a basis for correct behavior? Unfortunately, different countries may define things differently. Under some regimes in the past, and even today, it is defined as wrong to confront the behavior of the leaders. The 1989 massacre in Tiananmen Square in Beijing is a good example of what can happen. So is the brutal repression of people by the Ba'athist regime in Syria in 2012.

Human approaches to right and wrong

It is a deep human feeling that certain things are good and right and desirable, while others are bad and wrong and repulsive. Few people can live

1. Brown, *Philosophy and the Christian Faith*, 82.

without such opinions, and yet they have such difficulty deciding what precisely is right or wrong. Is robbery wrong? Then why does Robin Hood have such a following in English folk lore? Is murder, and conspiracy to murder, wrong? Then why do we think so highly of those who plotted to murder Hitler?

Perhaps it is possible for large numbers of people to agree on something. This is called democracy. Is it therefore right? Not necessarily. The death penalty is in force for certain crimes in some countries. Large numbers of people hold strong views for and against it. So is it right or wrong? You tell me. Or to take another example, pedophilia is perhaps the most abominated crime in Britain today. Yet in some ancient cultures it has been viewed as acceptable.

The difficulty over what is right and wrong stems from one central fact. Ultimately it all has to be defined by people, and people may be right or wrong in their definitions of right and wrong. Constitutions, legal systems and precedents, enactments of parliaments, separation of justice and politics: these are all human activities and hence capable of error.

Trust in a world of human error

Gradually, we perceive that human beings are not wholly trustworthy. However hard they try, they make mistakes, and this includes those who are nearest and dearest to us—indeed, since we see more of them, we know more about their capacity for error! We shall come back to the question of right and wrong later on, but for now, let us take a brief look at one other human effort to find something which is trustworthy.

Because human beings are often unreliable, some people look outside the human race for something which can be trusted. I am not thinking about those who try to contact extra-terrestrials or spirits, but of those who consider material phenomena as their starting point for an answer to the question of values. Some try to base their values on reasonably established truths, for instance. They may take a fact and turn it into a rule for behavior.

Basing rules on facts depends on what the facts are

One example of this is when people say rightly that some things are damaging to the environment and then assume that we should necessarily eradicate them. But throughout the history of the earth there have been damaging things which have not been eradicated, and which have disappeared for other reasons. Present concerns about global warming are as nothing in comparison to the anxiety which would be raised by the advent of a new ice age, perhaps covering most of the British Isles. Yet the last ice age only ended some twelve thousand years ago, and the fertile minds of glaciologists are replete with ideas about how the next one could happen.

Furthermore, human beings are part of the environment, so perhaps we should include their activities within our consideration of what is right and wrong. As a result, the matter is far more complicated than it appears at first. Eradication of all but "organic" farming methods, for instance, might doom a huge number of people to death by starvation. What started as a cozy "right or wrong" scenario about "chemicals" becomes a far more complex matter of finding the right balance in human activities. Science is moving, and if we try to define values this way, we have to keep redefining them.

How, then, may we find out what is trustworthy and what is not? There is no simple answer to this question, but the fact that it has arisen is an indication of the very big problems which face all human beings. There is no way to live without trusting someone or something. Consequently, we all answer the question somehow, but the answers could be desperately wrong. As with our consideration of naïve experience, there are no rules by which we decide what to trust. We have to start by making assumptions or axioms or presuppositions. And how do we know we are making the right assumptions?

5

Limits: space and time

What are the implications of being limited?

WE ARE OFTEN so concerned about freedom that we do not particularly notice the permanent limits which surround us all. The something which we experience has powerful, built-in limits. Athletes may continue to break records, but the margins by which they do so become smaller: there are heights which no high jumper will ever reach, and there are speeds which no runner will ever exceed.

In this chapter, we are concerned with the ultimate limits to which all human beings are subject. In general terms we speak of space and time, a four-dimensional reality within which we appear bound. The latest thinking of some mathematicians and physicists upgrades this common view to a ten- or eleven-dimensional reality, but we need not worry about this; dimensions, however many there are, imply limits to human ability.

If we are like those human beings who have lived before us, our time will reach an end, which we call death. Thus we are limited also in space, because we pass through time as we travel. Our size is also limited, our ability to do many things at the same time is limited, and even our ability to think is limited, though human beings have amazing achievements to their credit.

The solipsist's inconsistency

In passing, we may note that limits are the answer to the solipsist, who views all reality as the product of his own mind. If that is so, why is he subject to limits? Surely his imagination can overcome them? It is not surprising that there have been few solipsists: they find it hard to live with the contradictions between their philosophy and the real world they are forced to live in. Only suicide may release them from this tension, and then again, perhaps it may not: no one can come back to tell them what lies beyond, because they do not believe there is anyone else.

Perhaps then, we may decide that solipsism is not a tenable view of life. The implications are very significant. Once I abandon the view that I am all that exists, I have to accept that there is a real objective non-me (something outside myself) which I experience. This in turn raises all the questions of where I came from, where I am going, and how I should act. I am subject to the fact of my existence within a continuum which I did not make, and which has rules of its own. And of course, there are those limits.

Ultimate limits

If we can trust the findings of scientists over many decades of observation and experiment, the universe we live in is limited, and likely to end. Einstein said that the universe was finite, and yet unbounded. You can in theory travel for ever through the universe without leaving it, yet it can be measured, and may have an end. We can understand this truth by thinking of the planet on which we live. The earth is a sphere which can be measured as around 8,000 miles in diameter, making it finite. Yet its surface is endless: if we set off in any direction, we can continue going on for ever, or until the earth itself comes to an end. Upgrade this picture to however many dimensions there are in the universe, and we can see how an unbounded object can yet be finite and measurable.

How might the universe end? Currently, there are at least three possible scientific answers to this question.[1] First, the universe probably began with a big bang, and its expansion from the cosmic singularity, as the superdense start is called, is slowing down. It is possible that the forces of gravity may eventually bring everything back together in a *big crunch*. However, this possibility is not the view of many scientists at present, and another view is that the expansion will simply continue.

The idea of permanent expansion also has implications in view of the finite nature of the universe. If expansion continues, then eventually at some far-distant time, all energy will be exhausted, and an enormous emptiness will be all that remains, with the simplest forms of basic matter or energy in it. Matter is concentrated energy, and perhaps the latter is all

1. National Maritime Museum, "The Universe."

that will remain at the end. This idea is called the *heat-death* of the universe. Recently, an interesting variation on this theory was made by Sir Roger Penrose, who suggests that when the ultimate heat-death occurs, for various reasons, there may be a new big bang with a re-birth of the universe.[2] Perhaps this is what happened before the big bang of our present universe.

One other possibility comes from the finding that matter can change into different forms and that complex matter may break down into simpler forms. It is possible that the very building blocks of the universe, stable matter like protons, may even break down before the big crunch or the heat death can occur. This view may be called the *disintegration* theory.[3]

Lesser crises

Even before the universe comes to an end, there are other crises which may hit this planet and all its life, including human beings. Our sun, according to the best calculations, is about half-way through its life. In another five billion years the sun will expand to become a red giant star, and our planet will simply shrivel up and die.[4] Of course, some people predict crises before this, if our planet is not treated differently by human beings, or if it is hit by a large asteroid or a comet. In short, there is no shortage of potential crises!

What should we do if faced by one of these lesser catastrophes? Some suggest that the human race should spread to other planets. But it is not easy to find a suitable planet. The earth is just the right size and the right distance from a sun of the right size and has just the right conditions for support of its life. And anyone who would like to go on a space search for another planet must face two problems: first, space is immense and expanding; and secondly, perhaps we might not be able to find such a planet.

The nearest star to our sun—*Proxima Centauri*—is so far away that its light takes four and a quarter years to reach us. Is it possible that we could even find the energy needed to travel to its system? So far, manned space flight has consumed enormous amounts of our resources to send a few people to the moon, from which light reaches us in about one and a quarter seconds. How do we travel a distance over a hundred million times as far, just to get to the next star and any suitable planets it may or may not have? Is there enough usable energy available to us even to power such a

2. Penrose, *Cycles of Time*.
3. Board on Physics and Astronomy, *Hidden Nature of Space and Time*, 45.
4. Moore, *Atlas of the Solar System*, 74–75.

Limits: space and time

flight? If it were a manned flight, could we give it appropriate life-support systems? Multiply this problem by a few million more, and the complexity of a star-hopping search for planets will be apparent!

Sooner or later as we consider such questions, honesty, or even fear, may constrain us to ask what our existence is all about. Is this complex and often beautiful world a prison in which humanity is compelled to die? Will it all disappear without trace when the sun expands? Even if some of our descendants manage to make the unimaginably difficult journey to other star systems, will any of them find a planet on which to continue the human race? And even if they do, what of the eventual demise of the universe itself? What meaning can we find in life if everything is doomed to destruction?

Implications of ultimate limits

Because everything that surrounds us is finite or limited, it is possible for us at least to imagine something which is not limited, and which is infinite. In human terms, we can picture this something as existing outside the universe we know, though such a perception may not be strictly accurate. The infinite may have contact with this finite universe, and even pervade it in various ways, simply because the infinite is unlimited. This might be visualized, for instance, as water pervading a sponge, or as a map being consulted by a person. Both are involved with the object in question, yet they are not a part of it.

In view of the projected future of the universe, search for an infinite becomes important if there is to be any meaning in human life. If life, in Macbeth's words, is "a tale told by an idiot, full of sound and fury, signifying nothing," then Macbeth's behavior is as valid as anyone else's, and there is no way we can say that any form of human behavior is right or wrong. If it is all doomed, why not behave as you wish, as long as you can get away with it?

This was very clearly seen by the Marquis de Sade, whose views may be summarized as: "What is, is right." Of course, as modern thinkers might say, we do not have to behave badly all the time, but then there is no way such behavior can be viewed as wrong. It is all a matter of human preference. Thus pedophilia and rape, which are viewed as disgusting, cruel and barbarous in modern British society, were accepted and practiced at times in some great civilizations of the past. But people who have followed de Sade's views, such as the "moors murderers" Ian Brady and Myra Hindley, were locked away with no possibility of parole or forgiveness by British society even thirty-five or forty years later.

The helplessness of law

Thus, because no human judgment can have ultimate meaning in a finite universe which is due to end, law itself has no meaning. This has the most serious implications for all human behavior. It is the reason why our laws have become increasingly determined by sociological considerations. Whilst not necessarily wrong in themselves, such considerations are essentially arbitrary. Thus what is deemed right in one society may be deemed wrong in another.

This breakdown may be seen on both sides when we consider the environmental issues of our day. On the one hand, some people see nothing wrong in making their living from using resources in a way which may be legal but damaging to the environment. On the other hand, other people may oppose them to save the environment, but in ways that are illegal. In the finite, doomed universe which deprives all human action of meaning, neither group can give a universally valid reason for its actions. It is again all a matter of preference.

A startling recent example of the effect of variations in law occurred in 2002, when some people were charged with conspiracy to defraud the authorities at St Paul's Cathedral in London.[5] Two of those accused fled to Florida, where conspiracy to defraud was not recognized as a crime. Because of this, extradition could not be pursued, and in fairness to the other defendants, the case against them was dropped. What is wrong in one place may not even be seen as a crime in another place.

Human law becomes the arbitrary decision of those in power. In some places these people may be benevolent, but in the former Soviet Union, this resulted in countless cruelties and atrocities against huge numbers of people, as documented by writers like Alexander Solzhenitsyn. When law cannot be derived from what actually exists, there are tremendous implications for everyone. In such a situation, those who suffer have no rights: these are a part of law, and law is not absolute and unchanging, but has become one more thing which is decided by human opinion.

---

5 BBC News, "Trial Collapses."

Meaninglessness leads to the arbitrary

In this chapter, we started by exploring the limits to which everything is subject. We might call limits a form of law which everything has to obey. If the universe is doomed in one way or another, this brute form of law indicates that there is no escape and no ultimate survival, not even in terms of history because that will also disappear. Outside this there is nothing we can know, or which can know us.

Why, then, should any one form of behavior be preferable to another? To avoid the retribution which others might bring against our actions? Then we are saying that human opinion rules. It is "their" opinion against "ours": the opinion of a parent against a child; the opinion of those who have power against those without it; brute force in the last analysis determines law, right and wrong.

Not only does any absolute idea of right and wrong disappear: so do all those values and behaviors which have been admired throughout human history. Love, bravery and kindness become equal to hatred, cowardice and cruelty. We cannot escape these implications if we live in this universe which is doomed to die . . . unless the universe is not everything that exists.

6

The framework and the flesh

The importance of understanding the universe we live in

MOST OF US CARRY frameworks in our minds about the world we live in. Our lives are governed by order, and sometimes our biological bodies demand it. Traveling in a jumbo jet half-way round the world, our biological clocks rebel and take time to catch up with the change to expected rhythms. Going east, the problem is worse than going west, probably because we can absorb extra hours of rest more easily than we can do without it: days and nights become shorter when traveling east, and longer when traveling west.

Other frameworks may be systems of classification, such as when we decide that a creature in the distance is a fox rather than a dog, or systems of preference, when we decide that we will vote a particular way because of what we believe about the candidates for election. There are many possible types of system, all reflecting the way we derive unity and diversity from our experience.

Space-time and matter-energy

In this chapter, because we are thinking about the entire universe, we need to look at a special system which as far as can be seen, embraces everything in the universe. It is the system of space-time. We need not worry about how many dimensions space actually has, because this is something we can understand more simply! Space has a meaning for all of us, and so does time. The interesting point is that the two are wholly interconnected. Move

The framework and the flesh

through space and you move through time as well. And even if you try to stay motionless in space, parts of your body do not. So movement through time means you will move through space.

Now comes the interesting part. You are made of matter of various sorts, and energy is at work in your body. More than that, we have already noted that matter is really concentrated energy. The amount of energy represented by a small amount of matter is enormous, and that is why nuclear power exists. Indeed, nuclear reactions only release a tiny amount of the energy available in the matter used as fuel. So we can speak of matter-energy.

A long time ago, some of the scientists working in this area began to think of the question of what is fundamental in the universe. And if you think of a universe made only of space-time without any matter-energy in it, a problem arises. How can you speak of space? Well, you measure it. And how do you speak of time? Similarly, by measurement.

So far, so good. But how do you measure space or time in a universe without matter or energy? Think about it. The dimensions of space and time relate to the actions of matter and energy in the universe we are in. So if there were no matter-energy, there might be no space-time either. This was when some of the scientists became quite innovative. They realized that if space-time could not do without matter-energy (and matter-energy certainly can not do without space-time), then perhaps the two entities were interrelated.

One ingenious idea, which may be true, is that matter-energy is actually the product of space-time. The mathematics certainly fitted, and it could be represented by a picture which we can understand—as the ocean wave of space-time curved more and more, the foam of matter-energy was produced.

Other major frameworks

In a sense, all the frameworks of science may be traced back to the framework I have just described. We are talking, of course, of the science of physics. The two extremes of the spectrum of physics may be seen in cosmology and astronomy at one end, dealing with the big questions of the nature of the universe, and particle and quantum physics at the other end, dealing with the tiniest things we can study. But if we want to talk of chemistry, then we enter an area of greater physical complexity dealing with atoms and molecules, and to speak of biology we need to take the level of molecular complexity further to deal with self-replicating molecules and features of living cells.

In this way, it may be seen that everything we experience can be linked together in a gigantic ordered assembly. Of course, we do not understand it all yet! But there is every prospect that scientific frameworks may eventually encompass the whole of the reality which we experience. This is not the same as saying that we shall know everything, but rather that we shall have a knowledge of all major aspects of our experience comparable to knowing the bones which make up the human skeleton: there is an immeasurable amount of detail in the flesh on those bones! It is highly unlikely that we shall ever know exhaustively what happens in that flesh.

It is at this point that we may feel either very satisfied, or slightly uneasy, or perhaps both. We are satisfied, yes, because knowledge is good, but uneasy because there are aspects of our experience which do not fit into such a scientific framework. Music can be explained in terms of mathematics, and its effect on the emotions in terms of physiology and behavioral sciences, but the experience of music may be quite impossible to describe in such terms. Similarly with the visual and literary arts, what makes one poem or picture profound and moving, while another may bore us stiff?

We should appreciate therefore that though science is good and helpful in its own right, it cannot provide a description of all that we experience. The word "science" comes from the Latin *scientia* which means "knowledge." Acquiring knowledge is of course a human activity, but not all types of knowledge are what we call science. Underlying all science is the discipline of mathematics, which is needed for measurement and for making judgments about our scientific actions.

Preferences distort frameworks

Distortion of scientific frameworks is a commonplace event. People want the advantages of technology which come from scientific knowledge, but they may try to incorporate some other items which they happen to like. When I was at school, I heard a boy say that when he grew up he would like to be a school road crossing guide, a job often given to retired people, because then he would not have to work until he was sixty-five! I am not sure who he thought would keep him until then, but it illustrates how our hidden desires may guide our preferences.

So it is with science. We want the convenience, but we try sometimes to incorporate the incompatible. There is a romantic view that "organic" farming is the only "correct" way to live. The arguments against this are enormous, in the shape of the world population, and the fact that this form of farming proved a failure some six hundred years ago, when the population of Britain stagnated at three million for over a century.[1] This was because the soil had become depleted of some essential nutrients.

All farming is technology

Farming itself is, of course, a human technology. Before farming, there were people who hunted and gathered their food. Indeed, the hunter-gatherer culture itself persists today in some places, and the most widespread example is probably fishing. But we should realize that there is nothing that makes "organic" farming intrinsically better than any other farming technology. Indeed, the consequences of its adoption might be widespread starvation.

In parts of the world where it is the only farming technology, people are often on the edge of famine. With direct genetic modification technology, there is some hope for these millions of human beings. Even in Britain, which has to import some food, and where there is opposition to this form of technology, we feed 80% of the population with other forms of "non-organic" technology, as opposed to the tiny proportion who could be fed with "organic" farming. The reasons for this are that "organic" farming is wasteful of land, depletes soil of essential nutrients and produces food which rots quicker.

Rachel Carson and biological control

Of course, there are problems in chemical pest control, as Rachel Carson made clear.[2] But what is often forgotten is the last chapter of her book, where she pointed to the promise of biological pest control. Yes, she endorsed the research of geneticists, among others—work which has led to the development of genetic modification of crops in order to protect them against pests.

1. Emsley, *Shocking History of Phosphorus*, 235–53.
2. Carson, *Silent Spring*.

It is therefore important not to allow romantic or other hidden preferences to distort our scientific frameworks. Yet unfortunately this may happen in our society. Those with agendas based on persuasion of others may adopt all sorts of devices to try to achieve their ends. Of course the science needs to be accurate, and the technology well-based on that science, but there is no reason for the mindless vandalism of test crops by rural terrorists in the name of "organic" farming, as has happened on occasion in Britain.

Risks, advertising and human confusion

There are many other sources of distortion for the frameworks we live by. In the world we live in, it is natural for vendors to advertise their products. But products may sell better if the customer can be made anxious about the consequences of not buying. In addition, there are many self-organized pressure groups of people who think that their cause is totally right and should be supported by everyone. In such an environment it is easy for people to become confused and anxious. What are the ways in which we may guard against this?

One way is to ensure that we have a firm grasp of what knowledge there is. But unfortunately all knowledge has come into question in the present age. Not only do we have the benefit of the greatest accumulation of human knowledge ever to exist, but we are also exposed to the greatest flights of unreason which human brains have ever devised!

Side by side in the daily newspapers we see tolerable explanations of recent scientific discoveries and developments on the one hand, and things such as horoscopes on the other! Explanations of how a significant drug can help those who suffer from a serious disease are matched by advice from various "gurus" to use homeopathic remedies for common ailments. Homeopathy is a system which can only be true if all basic science is wrong. For instance, its "remedies" are supposed to have a greater effect if they are diluted.

Sometimes those who practise homeopathy also use herbal medicines; many herbal extracts are the basis for today's science of pharmacology, and in pharmacology, a stronger dose has a greater effect. To mix the two approaches is inconsistent and unreasonable, but those who do this seem not to notice the conflict in their actions.

The framework and the flesh

If we are to safeguard our brains, we have to make judgments about what is presented to us. We cannot simply accept all the unreason as though it is on a par with reason. Yet this is how the media in a "free country" usually function. Opposing "viewpoints" can claim equal time. However, it is often the unorthodox viewpoint which carries the greater fascination and steals the show! Those who found themselves bored with science at school actually may be attracted by something which appears radical and different. It may be useful to visit an authoritative website to help understand the problems with some forms of "alternative medicine," although there is no such thing in my understanding. Either a therapy works, or it doesn't; if it works, it is medicine, but if not, it is quackery. My favorite site is run by the retired psychiatrist, Dr Stephen Barrett.[3]

Is there a danger in believing the irrational, or even the highly improbable? Well, yes, there is if it provokes us to irrational actions. That is where chapter 2 started. How can we be protected from what is irrational? One important test of whether something is irrational is to ask how it connects with the whole of reality, so far as we experience it. Does the idea which is new to us actually work? Is it in harmony with all the rest of our experience?

Scientific laws and principles

This is where we move from a simple consideration of science to consider its basis. The principles on which human science is founded are sometimes implicitly questioned by those who wish to promote other views. For instance, scientists have a view of consistency throughout the universe. They believe that within the universe certain things are conserved.

If you hit a tennis ball with a racket, some of the energy in your arm is transferred to the racket and then to the ball which moves accordingly. This is part of the law that energy is conserved. Then also consider that your arm, the racket and the ball remain virtually the same throughout the action. This too is a law of science—matter is conserved. In terms of everyday experience, both are true, and can be verified.

However, when scientists discovered that sometimes in their studies of high energy physics, there was a small loss of matter and a large gain in energy, they had to change their simple view of what is conserved.

---

3. Barrett, *Quackwatch*.

Other studies also showed that matter could be formed from energy. Consequently, the two laws of conservation became one—that matter-energy is conserved.

This is a good example of how experiment and observation may lead to a better understanding. Notice that the laws were not disproved, but were brought together in a greater law which encompassed them both. Indeed, unless there is actual change of matter into energy or vice-versa, the original laws still hold. Much of the twentieth century's scientific progress has come from studying situations where a scientific principle seemed to be wrong. The result is invariably a deeper level of understanding and an even firmer basis for believing the accumulated wealth of human science.

The uniformity of natural causes

There are numerous scientific laws at the various levels of science, but beneath them all is one important principle which binds them together. This is the principle of the uniformity of natural causes. Broadly speaking, this is an acceptance that if something is done under a specified set of conditions at one position in space-time, and is then repeated under the same conditions at another position, the result of both actions will be the same.

If the principle of the uniformity of natural causes were untrue, there would be profound consequences. First, causality would disappear. We would no longer be able to do anything to bring about a given result. Secondly, science would disappear, since human knowledge is based on observation and experiment. Thirdly, chaos would prevail, and we would have no basis for living, since all our actions are based on knowledge of what has happened in the past.

In the strictest possible sense, *everybody* depends on the uniformity of natural causes.

The world which we don't live in

I have brought our discussion to this point quite deliberately, since there are considerable forces in these times which attempt to discredit science. Insofar as science is a human activity, of course it is liable to error. However, if we seek knowledge, nothing is outside science. Furthermore, the methods of science are universally applicable. We do not know everything, but some things we know are objectively true, and not a mere matter of human opinion.

There was a philosophy half a century ago called logical positivism. Its followers claimed to be scientific, and insisted that for something to be meaningful, it had to be verifiable. If there was no way in which an idea could be proved or disproved, then it was without meaning. This was quite an attractive idea, especially for some who cast a jaundiced eye on certain religious beliefs. It took a while for people to realize that the philosophy of positivism had condemned itself almost before it began, since there was no way in which positivism could be proved or disproved!

Then the pendulum swung the other way. There emerged some people who felt there was no basis for anyone to criticize anyone else's beliefs, no matter what they were. The idea was that since no one knows what is true, you could believe anything you like. (The appalling corollary is that if no one knows what is true, all science disappears, and we are in total chaos.) This philosophy went under the name of postmodernism. You could believe anything, as the saying goes, as long as you didn't do it in the street and frighten the horses. This also was a beautiful example of self-condemnation. Suppose you wanted to believe that postmodernism was totally wrong? That would be a perfectly valid postmodern belief! With postmodernism, objective truth has disappeared. Do you want to be postmodern? Then try stepping off the top of a twenty-floor building, in the belief that physics and biology are mere inventions of scientists; after all, you are free to have your own opinion!

Both positivism and postmodernism therefore shot themselves in the foot from the very beginning of their existence. They are equally untenable as total philosophies, because they deny their own foundations. They have no relationship to science, which is founded on the repeated shared experience of human beings and can be summed up in objective statements. These two self-destroying philosophies are a permanent lesson to us not to believe ideas which may sound plausible but cannot even be consistent with their own foundations.

Self-destruction is one way for a philosophy to show that it doesn't work. Another way is when it fails the test of the real world. A logically connected system of thought has no use if it doesn't relate to reality. Mathematics may look beautiful (I think it does), but if its figures do not link up to real things it is just a game. Solipsism was like this, in that it failed the test of limits in the last chapter: if reality is in essence my dream, then why am I limited in what I can do?

Self-destruction is essentially the result of unreason. Inner consistency is necessary for a thought-system to be valid. A built-in contradiction is one guarantee of invalidity. The test of the real world is the other important standard which theories have to satisfy if they are to be considered true. In the world of science, experiment has become an essential part of establishing what is true. In fact, experiment is central to everyone's understanding of the world, as we shall see.

The two pillars of understanding reality

Most of this chapter has been concerned with reasoning, with science and with its philosophical aspects. Logical coherence and consistency are matters which come under the heading of philosophy. This is one of the most important things for us to appreciate. Our naïve experience finds its expression largely in terms of philosophy.

There is a second pillar supporting the edifice of human understanding, and this is what we may call history. History is the sum total of human experience in space-time up to now. It is a wise statement that those who ignore history are destined to repeat its mistakes. Too often in the media, some distorted nonsense which was fully answered many years ago is resurrected as though it were true or unanswered.

Science comes under both philosophy and history. The observed phenomena of science and their interrelationships are a matter of philosophical truth, and the accumulated wisdom of human endeavor in this field, which includes experiments, is a matter of historical truth. This is the framework of reality: to be real, something must fit into both philosophy and history.

In the next two chapters, we shall take a look at reason and experience as essential human counterparts of philosophy and history. Both are necessary to interpret and understand the universe around us.

7

Reason: what is it?

The effects of reason on naïve experience

IN THE PAST FIFTY years or so, we have been made aware of many seemingly intelligent behaviors of animals. Gorillas have a vast array of non-verbal communications, ranging from looks to grooming activities; monkeys have a variety of warning calls which can distinguish between stalking big cats, snakes, and birds of prey; dolphins and whales call to each other as they swim; and birds have an amazing variety of songs and calls which we are only just beginning to understand.

What makes human beings different from their biological relatives? Indeed, is it possible to say that there is anything which makes us better or on a higher plane than the creatures around us? Some would perhaps say that animals are nicer, and not as devious! Others would say that animals, in essence, can do much of what human beings do. Are we intelligent? So are carnivores, from lions to killer whales, in the ways they trap their prey. Do we use tools? So do many animals, from some birds which use twigs to dig larvae out of tree trunks, to the lammergeier, which drops bones from a great height on to rocks to obtain the marrow.

Even the humble flatworm has a memory, and may be conditioned to react in various ways to learned stimuli such as a bright light or to find the way through a maze. What can we say is unique about human beings?

The uniqueness of human beings

Perhaps we can say that the scale of human actions is different. When we come to consider the nature of personality, we will identify some characteristics of which animals show little, if any, sign. But the one central factor which sets us apart is the scale and scope of human reason. We may see this in action in two principal arenas: analysis and creative activity. Analytical phenomena are apparent, for instance, in all types of descriptive science, philosophy and learning: we understand, classify and reflect. Creative activity is shown in art, music, literature and all types of technology.

What is meant by human reason? It is a faculty which depends on learning and experience, and which is used to control our environment. Historically, when farming developed in place of hunting and gathering what was needed for life, a better technology was thereby created to make life more certain. Even if you have the tools to make hunting and gathering more effective, the food supply may dry up, making the technology useless. With farming came the need to manage a changed environment, in which some insect pests, for instance, found a huge new source of food as a result!

So control had to be extended to include the pests, and some ways of control proved better than others. For instance, it may be preferable to insert a gene to protect a food plant against an insect, than to use some pesticides which not only poison insects but also the often more beautiful animals which feed on them. As mentioned in the last chapter, this was one of the implications of Rachel Carson's famous book, *Silent Spring*. Biological control may be better.

Control is one of the aims of human technology, and therefore of human reason. People try to control their own lives including food, clothing and shelter as well as many other things such as information, communication, transport and recreation. Often in the process they try to control other people too! We live in an intensely scientific age, in which every conceivable human activity has an associated technology. As one of my close friends used to say before he died, it is all part of life's rich tapestry. What it shows is the fertile creative power of the human brain in developing methods of control and with them, possible improvement of the surroundings.

Reason works on the material of experience

If we start from naïve experience, there are several ways in which we may turn it into knowledge. An *assumption* made from immediate experience may or may not be true, but it is usually the result of a rational decision. If we touch a nettle and are stung, the experience may lead us to assume that all such leaves sting, and of course this would be wrong in the case of the plant called dead nettle. Observations are the raw material for most assumptions.

Information may come from a *source* and to this source in turn we may allocate a level of reliability. When we consult a professional such as a lawyer or a doctor, we are inclined to take their advice, even if it means we have to change our opinion. In this situation we assume something, but with a possible reservation. According to a British Medical Association poll, journalists are viewed by the public as a poor source of reliable information, but doctors are much more trustworthy!

We may *deduce* a particular fact from a general law. For instance, if electric sockets carry an electric current, it is unwise to stick my finger into the next socket I come to. The mains may be switched off, but perhaps it would not be wise to assume this in the circumstances.

The opposite of deduction is the *induction* of a general law from particular facts. If I get an electric shock by putting my finger in a socket, perhaps this is because sockets tend to carry a current. Of course, there are many examples of deduction and induction in science. Induction usually follows a series of observations of a particular event, and deduction may involve putting several "laws" together to explain a new event.

Then we may devise an *experiment* to test any of these forms of rational knowledge or belief. This is the use of reason to create a new form of experience which is based on our previous experience. Reason and experience work together in much of life. Of course our knowledge may be true, partly true or false, and if we are wise, when evidence is very strong we may change our views. Now let us use reason to make some deductions from our naïve experience.

Deductions from naïve experience

Most of us would consider "nothing" to be a more basic situation than "something." The presence of "something" clamors for explanation. If nothing ever existed, nothing would require explanation because there would be no explanations! But a "something"—especially a beautifully complex universe like ours—raises the question of an origin.

Origins of something

Some people have asked whether the universe had a beginning. Most scientists would answer yes, and say it was the "big bang." But even if it did not, there is still a question of origin. "Beginning of the universe" relates usually to the beginning of time, but if we supposed for the sake of argument, that time were never-ending, that would still leave space.

And if we supposed that space also was never-ending, that would still leave ourselves. Put simply, the existence of "something" with any limits at all means that there is something which can be termed an origin. Only the infinite can be without an origin. For the solipsist, the origin of the universe would be his own fertile imagination. Others would see themselves as having an origin outside themselves. We shall consider the question of origins in chapter 14. It is surprisingly simple to state.

Thus, our naïve experience leads us first to deduce that there has to be some origin. What can we deduce from our other naïve experiences?

Order and its consequences

When we first considered order in chapter 3, it was apparent that it existed on many levels. Furthermore, there were relationships implicit in the order: objects could be grouped according to similarities and the result of some actions could often be predicted. This led us to the deduction of structure. Everything relates to everything else.

Limits are also central to structure: some things are possible and others are not. In passing, when we speak of a miracle, we mean that the limits imposed by order have been overcome, sometimes dramatically. Structures have *altered* as a result. We should not rule out miracles. They may come from a higher degree of order than we normally experience. But for the most part, our experience of life leads us to believe in consistency (the uniformity of natural causes; chapter 6) and what we call *law* and order. There is a structure in the order we experience.

The message in naïve experience

The cohesion, and yet distinct identity, of objects at many levels of our experience was expressed as unity and diversity. The relationship of objects to each other and to us is a form of communication. A flower may relate to us through our senses of sight or smell. People may relate to each other in many ways including both speech and non-verbal methods. The planet earth relates to us by holding us on its surface, and to the moon by holding it in orbit. What makes human involvement in relationships special is that we may understand the source of the message and something of the thoughts and feelings of other human beings.

Two sorts of relationship

Our exploration of reason depends on spatial relationships. All we have discussed points to the interrelationship of *people* and *things*. There is also a relationship of *events*. Events happen in various chains which we may call sequences. We are involved in space, and also in time. As we have seen, the two may not exist separately.

From our naïve experience of sequence, we may deduce the existence of something called time, though it is hard to define. Temporal relationships often involve ideas of causality. Objects are brought together in space-time events with various results. In our complex world, however, it is not always easy to identify the causal chain, as with the storks and babies in chapter 3.

Outside me

Finally, the naïve experience of where I end and where everything else begins is the point at which I can deduce objectivity. It is linked to my limits and my appreciation of much that I do not control, as we saw in chapter 5. Objectivity is important because, without it, there is no basis for any human activity other than introspection.

Reasoning

Now we may put this series of deductions together in another little diagram. It is very important to realize that we began reasoning on the basis of naïve experience. Without paying attention to experience, reason is sterile. Experience is our link to the real universe. Starting with reason alone, as some people try to do, is the best way to come unstuck. We may end up with a coherent philosophy which has little relationship to reality, and which is therefore useless as well as wrong.

NAÏVE EXPERIENCE	DEDUCTION
something	origin
order	structure
unity and diversity	relationship
sequence	temporal relation
self and non-self	objectivity

Even experience may be misinterpreted, as has been apparent with the replacement of theories over many years of scientific experiment. Newton's laws of motion were fine until the speed of light came into the picture. These laws are still a good approximation for speeds up to one-tenth that of light, but with modern high energy physics we need the developments from Einstein onwards. Now that we have looked at reason, it is time to look again at the matter of experience.

8

Experience: how do I understand it?

The effects of experience on our reasoning

EARLY LIFE IS FILLED with experiments. We are experimenting creatures. We observe from the cradle onwards, form hypotheses and test them. This is not to discount any inbuilt instincts. A baby observes a smile, and smiles in response. Soon there are lots of smile experiments, and adults like smiles, so they smile back.

Then the experiments become more complicated. They involve speech, gestures and activity. They take into account the approval or horror of adults, especially of parents, and eventually of children of the same peer group. Sometimes the experiments become more formal, as in science lessons at school. But always there are experiments.

Experiment is to test reason

Children frequently take risks. The risks are really experiments. How far can I push my ability? What is the limit of my ability? Can I jump across the muddy bog? Can I play a game and win? Games always test limits, and sometimes the limits expand a little: sport is all about limits and our ability to break them.

But underneath it all there is usually a hypothesis. Perhaps I can jump a little further than last time. Perhaps I can astonish my friends. Perhaps I can win. If I do, the hypothesis is proved, at least until next time. But if I don't, what then? The hypothesis needs adjusting. Either way, I can learn something. But some people never seem to learn. Some criminals always get caught. Some folk always do the wrong thing and suffer.

Reason is to build frameworks but experience may be shared

The trouble is that reasoning can be faulty. We need to check our reasoning with experiments, but we need to check the results of the experiments with reason. It's a two-way system that we use in life. We saw something of frameworks in chapter 6. And we saw that experience, which includes observation and experiment, is the counterpart of reason. Reason is something which can be viewed as timeless, although our view of it may alter with time. Reason can be dealt with logically. But experience is a matter of history. Our experience is our history.

Logic and reason are universal. With sufficient definition, they hold true for all people at all times. But experience is individual. It is different for each one of us. Yet if we are experiencing the same universe, there will be ways in which we can have much in common as well. Seafood is not a universal taste. But enough people like it for there to be seafood restaurants. To be honest, I like many vegetarian dishes. But I like them most with meat! And it is our experience which has led us to these differences.

So reason and experience are universal, though the reason should be something which we have in common, and the experience may be different for everyone. But what about naïve experience? This is so rock-bottom that we may perhaps all share the same perceptions at that level. At least, that is what I am asking you to consider. Do you have the basic experiences, first of something, then of sequence, order, unity and diversity, self and non-self? If so, then in this sense, naïve experience is common to all of us, and has similar features in all our lives.

Experience is history and takes time

As we pass through life, our views may change. But usually, we hold to the same system of reason and logic. This gives us a point of contact with each other, through which we may have discussions. What makes our views change is our changing experience. The child who has a sip of wine may find it repulsive. But the adult who has learned different tastes in food may find a suitable wine to be an excellent accompaniment for a meal. Experience is linked to learning, and learning is involved with reason. But experience depends on the passage of time, while reason is formed into frameworks.

In what ways may our reason be changed by experience? The commonest way is when we repeatedly encounter something which appears slightly wrong by our current frameworks of understanding. This may be a factual statement in a book, for instance. Pluto has an orbit larger than the planet, Neptune, so we would expect it to be farther from the sun. Yet for part of its 248-year orbit, Pluto is closer to the sun than Neptune, which takes 164 years to complete an orbit. Finding that Pluto was sometimes closer to the sun led me to modify my teenage framework of the planets to allow a very eccentric orbit for Pluto, something shared by no other planet. Of course, Pluto now has been re-classified by the International Astronomical Union as a dwarf planet!

However, sometimes experience may be invested with false attributes. Many years ago I encountered some people who tried to substitute their "experience" for reason. They held views which were demonstrably wrong and tried to justify this by appealing to their greater experience of life. Now that I am older, I hope I don't do this myself! At least no one tries it on with me any more. Experience is useless if it does not work with the best reasoning available.

Two ways to "fix" on the truth

To fix a position on a map we need to give a grid reference. The commonest way is to measure where two imaginary lines cross, one running east-west, and the other north-south. We may also fix a position by giving directions on how to get there. Likewise, reason and experience may give us two separate ways of fixing a truth. If they disagree significantly, perhaps we should investigate whether the supposed truth is in fact untrue, or whether we have misinterpreted either reason or experience.

As we have mentioned, reason involves a logical framework, and experience involves history, often as we *experience* it. The clash of logical frameworks is most evident in public enquiries, where there is frequent mistrust, and polarization of people with different attitudes. In the "Bloody Sunday" enquiry concerning Northern Ireland, for instance, two sets of opinion clashed regarding who fired the first shots. In the absence of a satisfactory factual framework, and with controversy over the shared experience, such disagreements cannot be resolved.

However, if reason and experience agree, this is stronger evidence than either on its own. In a criminal trial where there is conflicting evidence from witnesses (experience), there may also be a logical framework of scientific tests which gives one experience-based view greater validity. In general, we tend to think of logic and science as more trustworthy than experience and history, for a variety of reasons. Experience is subjective, and so we regard it as error-prone, like people; science is still subjective, for it is the work of people, but it is open to testing by others and therefore has a sense of objectivity about it.

Where philosophy and history meet

In the eighteenth century, Gotthold Lessing, a German thinker of some note, maintained that "the accidental truths of history can never become the proof of necessary truths of reason."[1] Later thinkers called this "Lessing's Ditch." In this he assumed that history involved accident, meaning what is commonly taken to be chance, and was not on the same level as the logical systems such as mathematics which were true for all who used them.

However, order envelops everything. The very word "accident" describes something which is perhaps unintended or unexpected by human beings but nevertheless occurs according to the same natural laws which govern everything. Indeed, the occurrence of most accidents follows well-understood actuarial rules, and therefore an enterprising insurance industry can offer to protect you against the consequences (for a modest premium).

It is true that historians frequently seem to have difficulty deciding why certain events have occurred. For some events there is so little evidence that it even may be questionable whether they have occurred. We know that human beings may tell lies or go into a state of denial about what they have done. It is also possible to make mistakes in good faith. That is why we try to apply every possible cross-check to the most controversial events, those which may seriously affect the lives and welfare of many people.

Philosophy is about logic, laws and the nature of reality. History is about the sequence of change in that reality. In theory, if we knew absolutely everything about everything at one point in time, including the laws which govern it, we should be able to predict the future. But this is clearly impossible. So our forecasts are not certain. One of my nieces, a meteorologist, told me that we can predict the weather 12 hours ahead with approximately 50% certainty. After that, the probabilities apparently decline drastically. Prediction is uncertain, but what about the certainty of *past* events?

If the past is fixed and unchangeable, then it may be possible to identify reasons for some events by combining logic with historical knowledge.

1. Brown, *Philosophy and the Christian Faith*, 88.

Experience: how do I understand it?

As I mentioned before, this is the way in which criminal investigations and trials proceed. But in a trial, there are rules of evidence to prevent juries from jumping to the wrong conclusion. For instance, if the accused person has committed the same sort of crime before, this usually should not be mentioned, because such evidence does not prove that he is guilty of *this* particular crime, and juries might reach a wrong verdict. (In the UK, the Criminal Justice Act 2003 has made such evidence admissible under certain circumstances.) And as a scientist, I depend on the recorded experiments of previous scientists for my knowledge. If Lessing (mentioned above) were right, experimental science would have a very precarious foundation!

History is collected experience

Experience is a history. It is as much of the past as we can recollect, and therefore it may be deficient and sometimes inaccurate. But there are some things which we can check with logic. For example, taking the analogy of crime, if a man is accused of some offence at a particular place and time, indisputable evidence that he was elsewhere at the time will clear him. History and logic are dovetailed in all matters. An error in one entails an error in the other. Experience and reason essentially should agree.

In the sciences, this principle is central to all our investigations. What is expected on the grounds of reason may not always be true, because we have not taken everything into account. For example, observations of dietary habits have suggested that beta-carotene, an antioxidant related to vitamin A, may help to prevent heart disease. But carefully conducted experiments—clinical trials—have shown quite the reverse, namely, that *supplementation* of the diet with beta-carotene may in fact have an *adverse* effect on the heart.[2] Heart disease is a complicated matter, and experiment is the only way to test hypotheses based on such observations. Experiment is essential to test the "apparent truth" yielded by observation.

It is because our knowledge is far from total that we need experiments to test our hypotheses. Experiment is a similar word to experience, and indeed is a historical test of our reasoning. Today there are huge libraries of our experiments, part of the fabric of collected human knowledge. Every working scientist knows not only the reasoned framework of his part of science, but also something of the historical evidence of experiments which support it.

2. Egger, et al., "Spurious precision?" 140–44.

In conclusion, reason and experience are a check on each other. Similarly, philosophy and history are indissolubly linked in our understanding of reality. We need both if we are to understand our naïve experience. Errors may occur in our reasoning, or in how we interpret our experience, and also if we do not check one with the other. Together, they give us a powerful tool for investigation of reality.

Reason, experience and disagreements

The occasional apparent disagreements of reason and experience, either with themselves or with each other, are the sources of some problems which reach a high profile in the press. In general, there are two matters which should be examined when this happens. On the one side, reason may be affected by the wrong assumptions or even lies. On the other, experience may be misinterpreted.

Consider, for instance, the turmoil experienced over the combined vaccine for measles, mumps and rubella (MMR) since the infamous 1998 report in the *Lancet* apparently linking it with the development of autism in children. The report was highlighted in the press, and the response was predictable.

Some parents of autistic children wanted to blame someone for "causing" their child's problem. This was despite any other evidence to confirm the report, and plenty of good evidence against it. It is a good example of the power of a first impression, since the first they had heard of a possible cause for autism was the report. Afterwards, it would take a great deal to change their mind, even if this were possible. We might call this a misinterpretation arising from biased experience.

Other parents refused to have their children vaccinated because of the "risk," but what they obviously did not consider was the real risk (including death from measles) to which they thereby exposed their children. This attitude was fuelled in the media by certain adherents of "alternative medicine" who considered that immunization was wrong, despite the solid evidence of a huge amount of public health research. Their reasoning was based on the wrong assumptions, and disagreed with the results of experience in the shape of scientific research.

Still other parents who knew vaccination was a good thing wanted single vaccines rather than the triple vaccine, despite the evidence that these were definitely less satisfactory. Again, their reasoning was faulty,

Experience: how do I understand it?

since it involved a defective view of the evidence, namely a misinterpretation. More light was cast on this when a conflict of interest was revealed in the main author of the report in the *Lancet*. Most of the authors associated with the report, as well as the editor of the *Lancet*, publicly retracted it.[3] But even then, many people who had formed an opinion against the MMR vaccine were unwilling to change it, despite the fact that their opinion was based on no evidence other than sensational journalism.

Misinformation, selective experience and trust

Examples like these show us that there are many ways in which we can go wrong in the world around us. We should always be cautious when some new idea arrives on the scene, particularly if it conflicts with existing ideas or practices. It needs testing with both reason and experience. The first questions to ask are twofold. Is our reasoning based on sound foundations? And are we interpreting our experience correctly?

The noticeable thing about most real scientific discoveries today is that they agree with the huge body of science which already exists. This in itself is a strong pointer to their truth. Both reason and experience are in agreement. In 1930, Clyde Tombaugh discovered the planet later named Pluto (sadly demoted from full planet status by some leading astronomers early in the twenty-first century!). Tombaugh made the discovery because reasoning based on the observed motions of other planets had suggested Pluto's existence in the first place. Then he followed this up by painstakingly examining consecutive photos of the part of the night sky where the planet might be, until he found a tiny speck of light which moved in the right way. I have seen the actual instrument on which he did this in the Lowell Observatory in Flagstaff, Arizona. Thus observation-based reasoning was confirmed by experience.

But where reasoning is unsound, or experience is misinterpreted, there is no guarantee of truth. The total of human experience is often conflicting or confusing. In this context, naïve experience is clearly an important starting point, and the body of shared experience in "science" is often a good test for ideas. The matter of trust which we looked at in chapter 4 is also exceptionally important. Trust develops as we find both ideas and people to be *trustworthy*.

---

3. Horton, R. "A statement," 820-821.

A newspaper which publishes something we know to be wrong becomes less trustworthy in the future on those matters we know less about. A person who tells one lie becomes less trustworthy if we find out. We think less of a public figure who cheats his wife; he has proved to be less trustworthy. As we saw in chapter 4, life involves the risk of betrayed trust. We may build trust by confirming reasonable ideas with the tests of experience (experiments). It is clear that we do not have exhaustive knowledge on any matter. Nevertheless, it may still be possible to know real truth within narrow limits.

Taking the framework forward

We have looked at the two main avenues by which we try to understand our surroundings: reason and experience. We have also mentioned the significant matter of trust. Let us try to make use of these concepts, looking in turn at the basic perceptions of our naïve experience and seeing where they may lead our understanding.

PART B

Phenomena of naïve experience: the fingerprints

SO WHAT ARE THE fingerprints leading us to God? We have already looked at them briefly, but it was necessary to do some dusting with powder to show them up. Now that we have explored how we begin, we shall move on to what we experience. In one sense, all that we experience may be regarded as a message to us. How we understand that message, and incorporate it into our belief and behavior, has significant consequences.

After the first question—why there is anything—the next matter to concern us is order. Order may take several forms, so I have explored it under several headings. First there is the question of whether there can be any opposite to order. Does chaos exist? The very existence of "chaos theory" as popularized in the book *Jurassic Park* is enough to say no to chaos as a disordered state. What this complex branch of mathematics tells us is that there are many humanly unpredictable scenarios in the universe. Unpredictable does not mean truly chaotic; it simply means that we are not clever enough to understand all the factors and how they may affect a given situation.

After looking at order in general, we examine three aspects of order. First there is the matter of change, of movement in or through space-time and of causes and effects. Then we take a look at the most complex aspects of order in the nature of human personality. Finally the concept of unity and diversity is explored with special reference to communication, particularly between human beings.

If we so desire, we may treat life as meaningless, and ourselves as brute animals with no ultimate purpose other than self-indulgence in one form or another. But there is a cost in doing so which may become apparent as we proceed.

9

Something or nothing?

The something which is there, and its complexity

THIS IS WITHOUT A doubt the question which confounds us most. We can provide theories as to why one thing may give rise to another, and there are numerous ways of proceeding onwards from the big bang to the present time. But why is there anything at all? It would be easier to account for absolutely nothing, were it not that we would not be there to do so. Why have we a "something"?

The question does not stop there. Our experience is not merely of a something, but of an incredibly complicated something, which seems to act according to physical, chemical and biological laws. If this very complex something came from something simpler, then it also poses another profound question as to why it could develop from very simple beginnings. Indeed, most of us have heard of entropy, the tendency towards apparent disorder which complex things seem to suffer from. As complex systems proceed in their activity, occasional events (which we may call errors) gradually accumulate to destroy the system. The human body gradually accumulates these errors until the result is death, for instance. (As we shall see later, such "errors" and "disorder" are also part of a system of order, otherwise they could not be caused or have effects.)

The problem of complexity

It is possible to account for chemical or biological complexity in some places in the physical universe. We might argue that although the whole universe is in a condition of thermodynamic decay, nevertheless there are patches where the available energy allows for development of something of greater complexity. This is a reasonable argument, given the uneven distribution of complexity over the part of the universe known to us, but there is a far more profound question which is often forgotten. Why is complexity possible?

We may say, for instance, that the amazing result of the genetic code in human cells comes from exceedingly complex biochemical reactions; that these in turn come from simpler chemical properties; that chemical properties depend on the properties of atoms; that these also depend on the subatomic entities of which they are constructed, electrons (one type of lepton), protons and neutrons (both formed of quarks). These building blocks are held together by force-carrying bosons, mainly called photons and gluons.

Quarks, leptons and bosons in turn may come from yet smaller entities, but at the time of writing, there is no experimental evidence for these. We are saying in effect that the smallest items of matter (whatever they are) somehow produce the genes which control us. We may well wonder what is written in to the behavior of these minuscule things—which have never been seen directly—in order that such complexity can be possible?

Miracles for which we have no explanation

We do not even begin to have an answer to this question. It is analogous to the "something or nothing" question because no solution is in sight for either problem. In a real way, both of these questions highlight miracles for which we have no explanation. There *is* something, and there *is* complexity in that something. But can we account for either the something or the complexity? Try as we might, we cannot.

This is *not*, repeat *not*, a question about history. It is *not* a question about how particles gave rise to atoms, molecules and living organisms and how living things developed from simple to complex forms. These historical questions have all been given answers of a sort by scientific investigations. The question is *why*? Why is it possible for anything to exist? And why is what exists so incredibly complex in places? Is there something which (or someone who) is self-existent? If so, what is it (or he, or she)?

If the nature of our simplest experiences is inexplicable, a little humility would seem in order when we encounter the miraculous in other ways. For instance, some would seek to deny that Jesus rose from the dead on the ground that they have never seen such an event. But have they ever seen something come into existence where previously there was absolutely nothing? And yet the evidence for this is all around us. In the same way, how can we discount the physical resurrection of Jesus, which seems to be the only way in which the early church could have started from the small, sad group of followers who witnessed Jesus' death? The testimony of the writings in the Christian Bible is that they couldn't take in the resurrection even when he foretold it, and that when it happened, at first they couldn't believe it. We shall look at this again later.

Everywhere we look, there is evidence of the miraculous. Why should we find such *pleasure*, as many people do for instance, in music, pictures, books, food and drink, films and plays, holidays in distant places, the act of love, or the birth and development of a child? There is simply no explanation for this. To seek psychological explanations—if we can find them—is merely to raise the question of *why* there are such things as psychological events. Are these also written into the quarks, leptons and force-carrying bosons?

The implication of naïve experience

It is difficult to talk of an implication of our most basic experiences, but one is clearly possible. The quite extraordinary and amazing reality all around us carries its own message to those who experience it. This message we are exploring at present. If we say that our very existence as thinking, experiencing beings is *written into* the basic material of the universe, it is difficult to avoid the realization that our surroundings and identities carry some sort of message to us. We shall explore this at a later point in the book, but for the present we need to understand that we cannot ignore our experience without being irrational.

Put very simply, the existence of a something which includes ourselves as perceiving beings within it—made of the same building blocks, obeying the same physical laws—is evidence of a message to ourselves, the perceiving beings. It is telling us that there are things about ourselves and our surroundings which we can never understand by our own cleverness. It is a clear message to us that we need another approach if we are to find answers to the questions of why there is something, and why there is complexity. Because we are thinking beings, some of us may feel that we *ought* to be seeking such answers.

Despair and the police state

Of course, we may say that we accept there is no explanation of why there is something, and that we are not going to spend our time in fruitless exertions.

God's Fingerprints

We want to enjoy the life we have without seeking answers which may not exist, or which we may not be able to find. We may even say, as some do, that the brute, inanimate universe has always existed, and that we are merely a product of this entity. For the defects of this approach, see chapter 14.

I think, however, that I have already outlined why this approach may not turn out to be very attractive. The problems of human behavior mentioned in chapters 4 and 5, for instance, are no mirage. If we do not have human law and ethics rooted in a firm and real foundation, we have no answer to the crises of modern society other than the police state, and this is really the result of a philosophy of despair. Such states are effectively shouting out that there are no answers, that force is the only way to control the extremes of human behavior.

Some of us, at least, are repelled by police states, but they have a logic arising from profound despair about human behavior. In the aftermath of appalling crimes, we naturally want to make it impossible for them to be repeated. We also want our other societal structures to work without mishap. Consequently there is a huge and growing framework of surveillance and regulation of areas like teaching, medicine and finance. All these regulations are intended benevolently, and no one can see any alternative, but they are a further limit on all of us and present the possibility of control for its own sake if the "wrong people" gain the ascendancy.

Therefore, though ignoring ultimate questions may seem attractive, we need to pay some attention to them if we are not to create structures which may enslave us. It is time for us to re-visit the little diagram arising from naïve experience. This time, let us go on from the deductions made in chapter 7, and add a further column which we may label "opposites." These are not necessarily exact opposites, like black and white, but are more like the other side of a coin, the "tail" instead of the "head." The new diagram looks something like this:

NAÏVE EXPERIENCE	DEDUCTION	OPPOSITE
something	origin	void
order	structure	randomness
unity and diversity	relationship	uniqueness
sequence	temporal relation	separation
self and non-self	objectivity	subjectivity

Void: non-being

The presence of something leads us to consider how it came to exist and be as it is. Equally, we might say that it could lead us to consider the prospect of emptiness, or perhaps more accurately, the idea of non-existence or non-being. For obvious reasons, this is something which we are unable to experience, since all experience requires our being, or presence! Yet we are forced to contemplate the idea of non-being because of the presence of death in the universe.

Death, indeed, is a matter which few of us have contemplated in depth. Shakespeare gave one well-known view when he described it as "the undiscover'd country from whose bourn no traveller returns." How are we to regard death if not as an extinguishing of all we know, a cessation of our body chemistry and therefore of our thought and personalities?

Others have shown great anger against death—the great poet Dylan Thomas told us not to go into death gently, and indeed urged us to rage against it. This anger rests on the view that we matter and have a value now. Nor is anger the only possible reaction to death; anxiety instead may result from feeling undervalued. When Spike Milligan died in 2002, *The Times* reported that his greatest fear was of an obituary which would read "He wrote the Goon Show and died."

So what are we to say of the void? If it is all that awaits our personalities, and if the universe itself is destined to go the same way, then it makes nonsense of all that we do. Why do we have a life which potentially is so enjoyable and beautiful and interesting, if it is all to come to an end? Such is yet another of the questions raised by naïve experience.

Chaos and randomness

Many people consider that life can be chaotic, particularly if random events may affect us. If cancer strikes, the first question in some people's minds is "Why me?" Sometimes there may be a good answer to that question, such as: "You're a smoker" for someone with lung cancer, or: "You spent too much time in the sun" for someone with cancer of the lower lip. But then there may be other questions like: "Well, the same applies to person X but he hasn't got this cancer. Why me?"

At one level, it may seem that there is chaos. Cancer usually results from a number of genetic mutations which may occur through factors like smoking or exposure to ultraviolet light through sunlight. But there are other factors which may play a part, and the end result is that not all people with the known causal factors will develop the disease. Environmental and background radiation arises mainly from the sun and other stars and from radioactive decay of elements on earth. It passes through all of us and may be the final trigger of a cancer. It is difficult to pin this down as the "cause." You just happened to have a tiny bit of a particular sort of radiation hitting a tiny part of the genes in cells in your body. In the past four years, two of my close friends have died in less than a year each from the diagnosis of a grade four glioma. There are no known causal or risk factors for this uncommon tumor. It is probably a result of the background radiation to which we are all exposed on our planet.

But randomness obeys laws. We do not see these laws at the level of the individual who develops a cancer, but we can calculate the risk of developing a cancer, and this is what insurance actuaries rely upon when calculating premiums for treatment of disease. In any population they can calculate the risk of developing most cancers, and then they can add risks such as those caused by smoking or sunlight. What they cannot take into account is the risk of tiny events which affect everyone.

The basis of statistics is the way in which events occur. A single event usually cannot be predicted, but a group of such events can. We can calculate an average height, for instance, for a whole population, and also a measure of how the individuals in that population deviate from the average. Given this data, we can predict how likely it is that an individual has a specific height.

Similarly, we can calculate weight, and the relation of height to weight in something called the Body Mass Index. This in turn is related to obesity, and obese people have a whole range of risks which are higher than for non-obese people. Thus, from knowing about the whole population, we are able to predict probable risks for people within it.

These are examples of the laws followed by the mathematics of randomness. Randomness does not mean chaos. There are laws in every sphere of life. We will consider this more in the next chapter.

Uniqueness

Unique means there is only one item precisely like this. It might seem that identical twins are not unique, but they always have some differences, and sometimes they deliberately choose to emphasize their individuality in clothing or hairstyles! At a more subtle level, each person and even each thing is unique by virtue of a unique position in space-time. This is a consequence of the diversity which exists in the universe. Unity emphasizes similarity, but diversity emphasizes difference. Because of similarities and differences, communication is possible and necessary. Birds of similar species can communicate with each other because they share similarities, and they need communication precisely because they are also different, unique individuals.

Uniqueness is a quality which makes people feel that they have some significance, some importance and hence also some meaning. Each personality has a unique identity, and a unique role in the history of the universe. In the huge expanse of space-time, one small part is occupied (I might say *forever* occupied) by me. I am an indispensable part of what exists, and maybe I can influence part of it permanently. Self-actualization is viewed by psychologists as an important motive for some human actions. But this motive depends on the existence of a unique self.

Uniqueness means I am *special*. Some people are all too aware of this, and their actions and words can be off-putting to others! Conceit leads them to think they are special in a way other mortals are not. Uniqueness means we are *all* special. Other people at the opposite end of the conceit spectrum may have what is called a low self-image or self-esteem. This too is an error, but sometimes it takes more than reassurance to correct it. Those who have been told repeatedly that they are a waste of space (the immortal words of Basil Fawlty to Manuel in the television series *Fawlty Towers*)) may have difficulty in improving their self-image without prolonged examination of their own personality, sometimes with professional help.

There is a special angle on uniqueness in the Bible's opening account of creation and the beginnings of human history. Human beings are described as made in the image of God. That is, they share in some aspects of their creator's existence. People who believe this have a special insight into the uniqueness and preciousness of all human beings. At the same time, the awesome thought that they share some qualities of their creator should inculcate a degree of humility and forbearance towards other people and indeed all aspects of the universe.

Absence makes the heart grow fonder?

The sequence of temporal events clearly shows relationships between events which are cause and effect, but it also shows their separation. If two people in love have to spend time apart, it may increase their mutual affection. We are responsible for the results of our actions, but not to an infinite degree. Indeed we may hope that, given time, our mistakes can be put right. If two people have a child who grows up to be an adult criminal, the crimes are not said to be the parents' fault. Whatever the shortcomings of the upbringing, the child is another unique and *separate* individual, with a separate responsibility. Hence the parents are not admonished or punished for their child's crime when the child has grown up.

One significance of the separation of events is that although we may discern causal chains, we are not at liberty to attribute motives to actions without considerable evidence. Well-meant actions may have quite the opposite effect from what is intended, and good may result from some evil actions. We have to be extremely careful in judging the actions of others, lest our own actions prove to be wrong or ill-considered. It is much easier to say that an action is wrong than to say the person who does it is wrong.

Separation may have another significance. It may come as a message to us when we experience a marked discontinuity between events, one that makes us search in vain for an obvious cause for what we have experienced. I believe such events (miracles) are rare, but in chapter 11, I shall give an example of one which radically affected several people including myself. This will be further evidence that Lessing's view of "accidental events of history" is wrong (chapter 8).

The inner world of the mind

The experience of selfhood shows us what is the outside reality (hence objective), and it also shows us an inner self, a subjective world of judgments and presuppositions which we use to assess and decide on possible actions. We need to be aware of our own subjective leanings, particularly with regard to what is desirable.

If the evidence says that men should drink 3 units of alcohol (a unit is defined as 10 milliliters of pure ethanol) per day for optimal health, then an objective evidence-based decision would be to do that. However, the subjective leaning of many men takes them either to be teetotalers or to drink alcohol in excess. There are also a few who may be teetotalers because they are aware of their inability to control alcohol—this too is an evidence-based decision.

Just as the universe outside has a teeming complexity of order, so the mind has a great and complex subjective world. The prophet Jeremiah wrote in the Bible that the heart—by which he meant the central subjective decision-making part of us—is deceptive. This also is a warning we should heed. It is all too easy to agree with something because we want to do it, and not for any objective reason.

In one of the Goon Shows, the character Eccles (played by Spike Milligan) was asked whether he knew what he was doing, when he was plainly suffering a prolonged electric shock from equipment he was using. His answer was "Yes, but I'm willing to take a second opinion!" It may be useful for us to take such second opinions when making important decisions. Indeed, that is probably why committees are so well established in human activities. They may bring a touch of objectivity to what might otherwise be subjectively determined decisions. However, look in chapter 21 for a slightly wry story about a committee!

Conclusion: a complex something

We have reviewed the main features of the something which we experience, and it is apparent that there are many aspects to be considered. Some of these aspects may be more important than others, but they all need to be kept in mind as we move to examine the experience of order in the universe.

10

Order and chaos

The existence of order suggests that true chaos does not exist

We have already seen that complexity requires some explanation. Not only is it apparent that there are many levels of complexity, from the tiniest conceivable structures of which everything is built, up to the almost unbelievable intricacy of biological organisms and human behavior. There is also the fact that the very simplest level must somehow carry the information and properties which go to make up the most elaborate complex levels. Somehow, quarks, leptons and force-carrying bosons carry within them the potential for genes and brains.

Historically, people have made some mistakes about complexity. One popular notion is that "time plus chance" leads to greater complexity. It may do, but equally, it may not. In any case, it is not possible to have the popular notion of chance—something for nothing, or something that is not caused—in a universe which seems to run in an orderly manner. Indeed, what does the term "chance" mean? Is it simply another way of implying an accident? Some people talk about randomness in the same way as they talk about chance. As we have seen and shall consider further, randomness is an orderly matter far from the popular concepts of chaos and disorder. And although time allows for a greater number of causes and effects, what if they simply do not occur?

Order and chaos

An example of confused argument

Why there is something is a different question from *how* there is something. A very significant example of confusing these questions can be seen in the debate which continues sporadically even today over creation of the universe and evolution within the universe. As mentioned in chapter 1, some people seem to think that if you hold to one of these concepts, the other is automatically excluded, that creation renders evolution impossible and *vice-versa*. Apart from the desire of various people to score off each other, I cannot understand why that should be so, and I am a Bible-believing Christian.

I have already alluded to this matter in chapter 1. So, to recap, creation is a matter which falls into the area of origins. If you want to believe that God created everything else, the arguments which take issue with it are those which state that the universe came to exist in some other way. We shall look at these in chapters 14 and 15. But please do not oppose creation to evolution: the latter is a question not of origins but of history. We shall consider the biblical account of creation in chapter 20.

Look at it this way: if you think that evolution somehow avoids the need for an explanation of where everything came from, you have a strange view of the universe. Change within the universe is not an explanation of its origin. And if you think that God created the universe, that really does not rule out a whole variety of changes within its history. To hold that creation rules out evolution is like saying that there is no intermediate stage between planting a tree and sitting on a chair made from its wood. The tree growth, harvest and subsequent carpentry are ignored.

Everything has its place

So let us keep things in their correct areas. Creation is about origins, evolution is about history. Likewise chaos and order are within the realm of history. If there is a *something*, which we presumably can agree, its existence is not a matter of history but of origins. The state of that *something* as we experience it today—whether chaotic or ordered—is a matter of history. Let us take a look at this question about order, and complexity. As we touched on order when we viewed origins, so we shall need to consider sequence as we look at order. Complexity is an effect of change.

When a baby is born, a tiny new being has been created. For this to happen, events of almost unimaginable complexity have occurred, from the fertilization of the ovum onwards. Strict rules of chemistry and biology have led to the development of a new person with the potential of further development to an amazing level of intelligence and ability. Please don't laugh as you think of some apparent exceptions, because I'm not joking.

But when a human being dies, what has happened? Has there been a change to disorder? No, we cannot say there has. The event of death is the superimposition of another form of order, a situation where decay also occurs according to strict biological and chemical laws. If this were not so, the science of pathology would be impossible. If disease and death were a breach of the laws of order in the universe, we would not be able to study them. On the contrary, a great deal is known about the event of death and post-mortem changes. Sometimes this is important in criminal trials.

So everything is ordered, no matter how disordered it may seem to be. It is a question of the right perspective in a complex universe. Governing everything is a system of reason which we call logic. We have seen that reason and experience are linked.

The laws of "disorder"

As we saw in chapter 5, one of the ways in which the universe might end is called the heat-death. Every action in history is accompanied by some heat generation. In many chemical reactions, heat is generated. As the sun burns, heat is generated. We deliberately generate heat to keep ourselves warm. Heat is a form of energy. Where does it go?

In space, it can be very cold. As we move from the planets Mercury and Venus, which are so close to the sun that metals may be liquid on them, past the earth which with its atmosphere and magnetic field is quite protected, eventually we come to icy places like Neptune and Pluto. With the sun no longer close, temperatures may be near absolute zero.

Heat is essentially energy, movement of molecules and other small entities. In the sun and other stars, matter burns to give energy. Given sufficient time, the matter will largely disappear, and the energy will be dissipated over the huge universe. This is not disorder. It is one of the simplest forms of order. It is also the opposite of developing complexity.

For complex structures of any kind to develop, there must be appropriate energy. The energy which runs our little planet comes mainly from the sun. Given sufficient energy, complex chemical or biological structures may be formed. But there is always a tendency for some energy to be lost. If we boil an egg, usually we throw away the water. If we make a table, heat is lost from friction as the saw cuts the wood.

All of these events can be studied in the science of thermodynamics. Gradually much order is dissipated and heat is lost to our use. Chaos does not exist, but things eventually become simpler if energy is not put into them. We might say that the universe began with a big bang, and since then has become simpler overall. However, in pockets of this universe, the concentration of energy has been so great that huge complexity has been generated.

Disorder in the most complex structures

The most complex structures we know are in human beings. Mechanisms of growth, body defense by the immune system, the blueprint of the body encoded in the genes, and many other things are contained in each body. What does disorder produce in a human being?

At the level of the physical body, disorder produces disease. This is no chaotic event, but the precise effect of physical and chemical laws. A ray of background radiation hits a gene; the result may be a cancer or a developmental disorder. A well-organized invasion of the body comes from some well-ordered micro-organism, and infection results.

But the body has its defenses. Before a cancer can develop, the initial damage may be detected and dealt with. The invasion of a microbe may be repelled by several highly complex and effective defense systems. Again, order is the rule of the day, and any appearance of chaos is the result of our limited understanding. As we have understood more, so chaos has regularly retreated.

Lack of control is not chaos

In human behavior, we so often refer to events as chaotic. Our political systems are often trying to achieve the impossible, so naturally the result may be peculiar. As a regular commuter before my retirement, I sometimes considered train travel to be chaotic. But this is merely to use the wrong word. Train travel (or the failure of trains to travel!) is simply the accumulated result of many logical events. It is, in theory at least, totally explicable why I might be delayed an hour or so. (Of course, the train company might be so embarrassed by the actual cause of the delay that they have absolutely no intention of telling me what it was!) Order has not been lost, but human control has.

In theory, we might control many events. In practice, we do not have the resources. The UK National Health Service, which has attempted to do the almost impossible on a limited budget, has sometimes been criticized for not spending enormous sums of money on treating a single patient. With a limited budget, it is often possible to help many other patients with life-threatening problems that are less expensive to treat.

Everywhere we see the outcome of human systems which go wrong. Rail disasters, traffic jams, hospital budget deficits, young people committing horrific crimes, illegal immigrants, failing schools—these and many more result from lack of control. There are reasons which may be adduced for most of these complex problems, and they are not chaotic, but out of control. Chaos does not exist.

The most complex problems occur in the most complex systems

The human mind is sometimes beyond the understanding of human beings. This is where some of the most intractable disorders occur. Not only do we have the many very dangerous criminals who are kept permanently in prison, but we also have an array of people with severe mental disorders in secure institutions. We are not able to understand how some human minds work, but the effects are often predictable and at one level, we usually know what to do.

Again, a virus on the internet may cause incalculable damage to many computer programs. It is also acting as a logic system, otherwise it could not gain access. If it were not an ordered system, anti-viral programs could not deal with it either. All complex disorders are the result of control failure.

To give a further example, in one of the *Financial Times* top ten books of 2007, Kenneth and William Hopper described the near-apocalyptic crises produced in some very large American corporations because they appointed top managers from people who had no experience of the "shop floor," but had been "trained to manage anything" in a business school.[1] Chief Executive Officers with the MBA degree, from Harvard or other

1. Hopper and Hopper, *Puritan Gift*, 142–164.

leading universities, were appointed in companies when they had no hands-on experience of the work of those companies. This was a major factor in their decline and near-collapse. The Hoppers date the disaster in numerous companies from 1970 onwards, when the "cult of the expert" began to take over management. In the 21st century, however, many companies have recovered by reversing this damaging trend. Company failure is not a triumph of chaos; rather it happens usually because people have not learned the lessons of history.

The Hoppers state that the same trend in appointing managers affected the British NHS.[2] I have noticed that in the best-run British hospitals (including one I worked in for nearly 30 years), there are numerous qualified doctors, dentists and nurses who have worked many years in the hospital system and been appointed to top management posts. They have the knowledge to make the system work!

Chaos in the true sense does not exist

These examples may help to illustrate that there is no such thing as true chaos. There are laws which interact to produce all sorts of results we do not want, and there is disorder in many situations where we do not have control. However, the entire universe we experience appears to be governed by physical and other laws, and many of these laws are understood by human beings.

Because we may talk of order, and because this means things are intrinsically open to our understanding, we may also examine the matter of cause and effect. It is clear that if order was not something which holds universal sway, we would not even be able to talk of cause and effect, since events would be disordered and incomprehensible. In a real sense, the universe would be meaningless, and we might not even exist. Since this is not the case, let us take another look at cause and effect.

---

2. Ibid., 141, 219.

11

Sequence and consequence

Causes and effects, including one miracle

TIME PASSES. HOW DO we experience this? We notice changes in our surroundings and ourselves. Pregnancy gives way to the proud but exhausted mother and the new-born baby. Life also gives way to death in due course. As we move through time we also move through space. Even if we are motionless with respect to the earth, the earth is moving round the sun and taking us with it. But of course, if we are alive, there is movement within us: we are breathing, our hearts are pumping blood round our bodies, and many messages are travelling along our nerves.

Time is about change. It is also about cause and effect. It is also involved in the principle of the uniformity of natural causes which was mentioned in chapter 6. If we have learned from the existentialist philosophers, we may view ourselves as always existing in the present, on the knife-edge between the unchangeable past and the undetermined future.

But does time only move one way? At the level of complex beings like ourselves it certainly seems to. We can only grow older, like animals and plants around us and even stars. But at the level of electrons and other subatomic particles there is at least a possibility of travelling the opposite way through time. Physicists have studied a large number of *antiparticles*, of which the first to be discovered was the positive electron or positron. It was pointed out by the celebrated American physicist Richard Feynman over sixty years ago that positrons could be travelling the other way through time.[1] The mathematics fit, for one thing. And since then the understanding of antimatter has grown.

---

1 Hoffmann, *Strange Story of the Quantum*, 214–20.

Sequence and consequence

At our level, change happens in one direction

However, there are logical objections to time travel as it appears in the long-running television series, *Dr Who*, for instance. If the past is as undetermined as the future, the present also can be changed. This would be a truly chaotic system, if it could exist! Just when you think England has won the World Cup, everything suddenly changes because some time traveler goes back and gives his influenza to one of the footballers.

This would be a real recipe for the impossible and bizarre. The stability and order which is so apparent in the universe would disappear, and nothing would be fixed. It is questionable whether such an existence is even possible. Certainly predictability would suffer some changes, because new causes could be introduced to alter effects way back in the chain of events, and then of course, these new causes could also be altered.

The point about change is that it all happens according to rules. At times we may call some such rules laws. Sequence is a further example of order in the universe, and we may view its effects as a sub-group of order. It is because of the irreversible nature of our existence that we can talk of our origins, because we look back in time to the beginning. But even if there were no sequence in a universe or system, the question of an origin would still be valid. It might not change, but where did it come from?

Did space-time have a beginning?

To say that everything in the universe comes from somewhere is to restate the scientific principle that matter-energy is conserved. It is slightly different to say the space-time matter-energy universe itself somehow came from somewhere, something or some person. We are unable to imagine anything outside the space-time of our universe in terms other than those of space-time. Thus to speak of a beginning is to introduce an idea which may not be applicable. If there was no time before space-time, how can we speak of a beginning to space-time? The time-honored illustration of a map is one way to understand the essential idea.

If the map represents the universe, and its two dimensions represent space and time, then we are viewing the whole of space-time as a permanent, fixed panorama. However, it is possible for us outside this artificial "universe" to contact any point on it and even to alter it. Similarly, within our universe, we can only operate according to the rules, but there is no way we can rule out possible "outside" influences.

"There is nothing outside the universe"

In a recent book, a physicist suggested that there was nothing outside the universe.[2] He apparently thought that scientific knowledge could not relate to anything existing outside, and probably intended to oppose the un-evidenced idea of other universes. He also stated that he did not intend to exclude religion or mysticism. But since we know no way in which we can go outside the universe and return, his hypothesis cannot be tested. At least, it cannot be tested in any scientific way by human beings, and he rightly called it a principle of cosmology. However, he then stated that this meant the universe was a closed system, and I would like to challenge this assertion!

There is only one way that I can imagine this hypothesis being rejected, and there are no ways in which I can see it being accepted. To accept it, somehow someone would need to show that there is literally nothing in existence except the universe. How do you look outside a windowless house and "see" absolutely nothing? You can't. But the hypothesis could be rejected if someone or something outside reaches in and alters something, or in my terms, creates a causal separation or discontinuity, particularly at a high level of complexity. But this would be a miracle, I hear you say. Absolutely.

Frames of reference, miracles and a miracle

The problem with miracles is that everyone seems to want either to accept them or to explain them away. There is a human belief problem about them which doesn't depend on whether or not they exist. I once heard a story about a man who thought he was dead.[3] He went to his doctor, who sent him to a psychiatrist. The psychiatrist said "I think you need to see some people who are really dead. Take this pin with you and stick it into every dead body you see. Dead people don't bleed." So the man went to mortuaries for a few weeks and stuck the pin into lots of bodies. When he returned to the psychiatrist he said, "Yes, you've convinced me. Dead men don't bleed." So the psychiatrist stuck a pin into the man's arm. The man went a funny color, and cried, "So dead men do bleed, after all!"

---

2. Smolin, *Three Roads to Quantum Gravity*, 17–25.
3. Montgomery, *Suicide of Christian Theology*, 122.

Sequence and consequence

This story is about belief. If you have a really fixed unmovable belief, it may be impossible to give you any evidence which will alter it. If you believe that miracles do not happen, no one is going to convince you. Yet I have to say that I once witnessed an event which I cannot describe in any other terms. It was a clear abrupt space-time discontinuity, an event which could not possibly be described in terms of space-time matter-energy cause and effect.

Most children begin to walk around 12 to 15 months of age. By the time they are 9 months, some can be held standing up on their legs. One of my daughters was unable to do this or anything like it. In fact, she had a problem with one foot. Instead of standing, she knelt. The problem was known before her first birthday. She was seen at a Manchester children's hospital by orthopedic surgeons, who said she would need two or three operations by the age of 5. In the meantime they arranged physiotherapy. She was very unhappy with this; she screamed because it was so painful. And she never rose onto her feet. Kneeling was all she could manage.

By the time she was over one and a half years of age, we were used to the situation. Yes, we were Christians. Yes, we prayed about it. But we never in our wildest dreams expected anything other than what the surgeons had predicted. One Sunday we had just returned home from church, and my wife went to see a Christian friend round the corner about some matter. Our daughter then got up on her feet and ran round our garden. It was so natural that at first I didn't notice what had happened. I said, "Do that again," and she did.

The problem had gone. We kept the next appointment at the hospital. No one could explain what had happened. To explain it, you would have to explain how a physical abnormality of a child's foot suddenly disappeared into thin air, and how a child who had not even stood unaided, let alone walked, instantaneously *ran*, a behavior which most children take several months to *learn*.

Perhaps you might say that the diagnosis was wrong, a view which I doubt because of the physical signs and the great difficulty in putting weight on her foot. But can a child of parents who were not even expecting a miracle somehow know that it is time for her to go from *kneeling* straight to the behavior of *running*, without even learning first to stand independently, and then to walk? At that age there can be no possibility of a psychological influence somehow creating such behavior, even if that were possible later in life. The simple and obvious explanation was that God had stepped into space-time and performed a miracle, and we accepted this explanation gratefully and thanked the wonderful God who did it.

I would like to point out in passing that there was no hype, no service at which someone claiming to have a gift of healing did anything for our daughter. Furthermore, I still believe that miracles are very, very rare. That is the only one I have witnessed for certain. I have heard of one or two others in over 50 years of being a Christian. I have also read a fascinating article in the *British Medical Journal* about healing miracles described by the historian Bede in the seventh century, and parallel miracles on the twentieth century mission field.[4] The author, a consultant obstetrician, documented them in some detail.

The miracles of Jesus

One further point of considerable interest for Christians is that no one attempted to write off the miracles of Jesus as though they never happened. Even the Jewish historian Josephus accepted that he was a "wonder-worker," and other Jews accounted for what they saw as undoubtedly miraculous works of Jesus by saying that he had a demonic power, an explanation which they found acceptable. Early Christians referred to his miracles as well-established facts known to their audiences. One interesting fact from the New Testament is that Jesus himself did not lay a great emphasis on his miracles. After all, he had a greater task in hand, as we shall see.

To write these miracles off today as though they did not occur is to reject some very significant evidence. Indeed, without the miracle of the bodily resurrection of Jesus, the early church could not have existed. He would have been another unsuccessful contender for the title of Messiah, similar to Simon bar-Kochba a hundred years later. But bar-Kochba was killed by the Romans in 135 AD, and there was no bodily resurrection for him. Have you ever heard of a world-wide religion named after *him*?

Discontinuity, separation of cause and effect

I referred to the principle of the uniformity of natural causes in chapter 6. Because this principle is universal in the space-time universe we inhabit, the occasional miracle will stick out in a way which will cause us great

---

4. Gardner, "Miracles of healing," 1927–33.

insecurity unless we are prepared for the possibility. Of course, when a miracle occurs, cause and effect are separated in one sense only. The cause of my daughter's healing was the action of a person outside this space-time universe. That person I and my wife already knew, and we also were bringing up our daughters to know him: the wonderful God who had made us and everything else. There is something and someone outside the universe; it is wrong to assume otherwise.

The law of cause and effect is so universal that we do not expect any variation in it. It applies throughout physics, chemistry, biology and all human activity. The very rare discontinuities are a reminder to us to remember the one who created natural law. But the uniformity of natural causes is a special form of order. Miracles, when they occur, are also ordered events. It is because they apparently introduce discontinuity that we find them unsettling, and perhaps they also upset us because we realize there is more than the space-time universe which we can explore and understand. Our frame of reference has to be large enough to comprehend things which we do not have any scientific ability to investigate.

It has been said that there are two versions of the principle of the uniformity of natural causes. We may specify that it takes place within either a closed system, like the physicist I mentioned earlier, or an open system. The closed system corresponds to the "nothing outside the universe" viewpoint, which as we saw, cannot be proved. The open system allows for outside causes to produce effects within the system. Miracles give some evidence that this can occur, but if you adhere to the faith that they are not possible, you discount the *only* scientific evidence that the universe is an open system. There is one other matter which is of considerable importance when miracles are considered. This is their origin. Who or what produces miracles? We shall look at this matter later on.

Ominous or benign?

It is worrying to think that we are at the mercy of cause and effect outside our control. Chapter 5 referred to this matter of limits. But it is even more worrying to think that there are causes and effects which are not only outside our control, but also outside our understanding. This line of thought has been explored in books, films and art. Goya produced a picture called "When reason sleeps, monsters are born," and C. P. Snow published one of his series of 11 novels in 1968 under the title *The Sleep of Reason*, inspired, if that is the word, by the infamous "moors murders" of Ian Brady and Myra Hindley.

However, things outside our understanding need not be threatening, but may be benign and kind. The problem is how to know. If we cannot see outside the universe, there is only one way to know a person there, and that is by the person reaching into the universe and communicating with us. We shall explore this a little in chapter 13, but before that we need to consider some more things within the universe—the questions of personality and identity. They are a further indication of the nature of our experience and existence. What is personality and where does it come from?

12

Identity and personality

Uniqueness and personhood

SCIENCE IS A MARVELOUS subject, but it is not the whole of life. With physics, we can understand how the basic building blocks of matter-energy cohere to give substances we call elements and molecules. With chemistry, we can understand the rules by which elements and molecules interact with each other and how the more complex substances are involved in what we call life.

Biology, the science of living things, extends from the control codes of organisms in DNA, through the function of numerous intricate tissues and organs, and into aspects of the behavior of plants, animals and human beings. But when we reach this point, there is more to appreciate than science.

Famous artistic achievements

Human beings are capable of quite amazing activities. They can create not only scientific achievements but also wonderfully moving artistic phenomena. Though there is a scientific side to everything we know, there is also a depth of emotion which can be released, entertained or harnessed only by literature, music and the visual arts.

The greatest of these works are quite unique—so original and distinctive that we may know them by the names of those individuals who created them. A Shakespeare, a Beethoven, a Rembrandt—the name conjures up a whole concept to those who have experienced the works in question. The style of such individuals is so exceptional that some writing, music or art may be described unhesitatingly by their names, and other works may be excluded from their life's work equally unhesitatingly.

Infamous achievements

There is a darker side, however. For every person who brings delight, there may be another who makes us shudder. In our own time, Alexander Solzhenitsyn wrote of the *Gulag Archipelago* where huge numbers of political prisoners suffered under Lenin and Stalin, and the cruelty of the Nazis and some of their allies was likewise almost unspeakable. And in this generation we have heard of the atrocities committed under dictators like Saddam Hussein and Gaddafi.

There are also frequent works of almost unspeakable atrocity against individuals in our so-called civilization. Vile crimes against helpless little children, and similarly against the helpless elderly, vie in the news with the use by cowards and bullies of weapons against those who have no defense.

The nature of identity

Individual people who have achieved fame or infamy may be well-known to many simply by their name. Thus the names Charlie Chaplin and Peter Sellers conjure up the ideas of comedy for which these people were renowned, and we might think of many in other fields of endeavor or entertainment. Identity points to the unique status of an individual, in these cases people, but also perhaps to a prize-winning sheepdog in trials, or to a newly-bred type of flower in a show. Identity selects the particular item from a group.

The concept of identity overlaps other related ideas. One of these is personality. We might say, for instance, that an identified individual is what he is by virtue of certain characteristics of his personality. What is personality?

The nature of personality

First, personality makes a division in the universe. The personal and the impersonal are dramatically different from each other. When a human being is so damaged in the brain as to be physically alive but without manifesting characteristics of personality, we speak of the "persistent vegetative state," actually comparing the being with a vegetable which is alive but

Identity and personality

impersonal. Sometimes we may likewise say of a favorite animal that it is "almost human," meaning that it is manifesting characteristics which we normally associate with personality.

There are some people who think that animals differ in no essential way from human beings, and should therefore be treated similarly. This is a point at which it may be difficult to distinguish between behavior chosen according to a moral code, and conditioned reflexes induced by rewards and punishments. Indeed, people following the views of the psychologist B.F. Skinner may believe that all human behavior is so conditioned.

So what does the idea of personality convey to us? Let us have another little diagram at this point. We shall look at some of the characteristics of personality and their implications.

PERSONALITY CHARACTERISTICS	IMPLICATIONS
self and non-self	recognition of subject-object distinction
identity	concept of self
memory	ability to learn
reflecting	ability to analyze and criticize
classifying	recognition of order
perfecting	abstract goals
expressing	creating, developing and communicating

Selfhood

The first attribute to consider is the distinction between that which is the self and that which is not. This may appear at first to be an easy distinction to make, but we have already mentioned the solipsist who does not make such a distinction. Then there are certain religions which view the goal of human destiny to be submergence of the self in everything else.

Is there any evidence that the self is unique? And what are the consequences of the view that the self is a problem and that it is better to get rid of it in some way, to overcome the difficulties caused by individualism, for instance? The first question is easily answered at the level of naïve experience; and the goal of reducing individualism has been embraced both by some religions and by some political views.

The unique self

Each of us, naïvely considering our own self, can say that it is a unique identity, unshared by anything or anyone else. It is an individual physical body, which may have the usual set of active components, or may be reduced by some form of trauma or surgery. It includes an individual ability to think, to which we give the term "mind," and the link between body and mind may be viewed in a number of ways: from the purely physical, where mind is a result of brain chemistry—to the purely spiritual, where the physical is viewed as a necessary or unnecessary encumbrance.

There is little doubt that the interplay between body and mind gives us much of our identity and nature. What we find physically pleasing may lead to mental argument in its favor! And the power of ideas to captivate the mind is also evident in people who accept much that might cause them physical discomfort. In the first case, there are those who rationalize unpleasant behavior such as stealing another's spouse; and in the second, there are many who have accepted one of the more self-denying religious or political views, either to satisfy their minds or to benefit others whom they see as deserving it.

Is the self a problem?

The interaction between self and non-self is frequent and all-embracing, yet the self is viewed as distinct by almost everyone. Thus we have ethical systems based on the ability of the self to be responsible, and political systems based on views such as "the greatest good for the greatest number." The carrot and the stick are integral parts of the reward strategies of both types of system, and the self is thereby viewed as an entity which may be influenced. This is the case even in those systems which consider the self in the most deterministic way, as solely the result of chemical reactions in the brain. The conditioned reflex still has to be conditioned!

So what can we say about the possibility that the self is a problem, that without its individual preferences we all would live in an ideal world? On the one hand it is impossible to deny the problem of conflict between human beings, but on the other it is difficult to envisage an ideal world without the many good things arising from individual differences. This two-edged sword is the root of the difficulties we encounter when trying to regulate human behavior: there may be great similarities between the

Identity and personality

abilities of both good and evil geniuses. Why do we have both types of person? It depends partly on how we define good and evil, and we shall examine this matter again. For instance, it cannot be denied that some (such as the late Osama bin Laden, for example) who are viewed as very evil by much of the world, consider themselves the precise opposite, and are so viewed by their bands of supporters.

So the self is a problem in many ways. Nevertheless, this is how we naïvely encounter the universe in which we live. There is no way in which the self can be abolished without abolishing people. Although we have no need to discuss the matter here, there have been many attempts to reduce the self's power, both by political systems, and by more individual approaches such as the use of drugs for people with behavioral disorders.

Inner and outer space

One very interesting characteristic of human beings is their ability to explore not only the universe around them, but also their own inner being and ideas and behavior. They seek to know more about themselves. With such understanding comes a greater ability to cope with the many twists and turns of life, and a greater self-awareness. Looking in a mirror helps us to know our appearance. It is interesting that many people marry partners looking like themselves. I have said jokingly that the reason for this is that most people cannot imagine anyone better-looking than themselves! It could also be that their familiarity with their mirror appearance conditions them to choose a partner with whose appearance they feel safe.

Identity is a matter of great significance to us. We are complex human beings and do not like other people to take over what we are, or what we do. Yet there is a huge industry based on imitation of the famous. Fan clubs and their associated paraphernalia testify to the enduring desire of many people to be like someone they admire. This is to bring together the inner and outer aspects of our existence. We may model our behavior on someone else.

The self therefore is a very important aspect of what we experience. Whether we are modest or conceited, humble or arrogant, we view the whole universe from inside the cage of the self, and our views may be colored by this unique experiential viewpoint. Our identity is something we start from in most of our judgments about the universe outside. To this we may add the accumulated experience of our lives, something which we could not consider unless we also had a memory.

Memory: the source of learning

Another characteristic of human beings is that they learn. Learning is not the same as conditioning. A dog may be conditioned to salivate when a bell rings, by linking the bell to food in its memory. In human beings, memory functions at an altogether different level. Our minds may roll around abstract and concrete ideas together, and come to significant conclusions about how we should act in a given situation.

Because we can remember, we can learn new things. Without remembering simple mathematics, for instance, we could not understand science which depends on logical relationships. Without memory, we could not speak another language. Virtually everything we do, from watching a film to painting a picture, depends on our memory. The memory is an essential aspect of the self.

When people suffer amnesia, huge changes can occur in their world. One of the beneficial examples of this is certain drugs which are used as sedatives. The benzodiazepine group, which includes diazepam, can cause memory loss. This means that all the unpleasant aspects of a surgical operation may be removed, leaving a calm relaxed patient on recovery. It can be good to forget some things.

Despite the fact that we often forget things, the memory is a powerful aid to coherence in our lives. Since, as the existentialists say, we live always in the present, the past is only in the memory. Personality depends on memory, as plants depend on the seed from which they grew. Without knowledge of the past, we have absolutely no idea about how we should face the future. Memory prevents life from being a terrifying series of experiments in situations which appear mad or chaotic.

On reflection

Reflecting is another aspect of our experience. We ponder or consider our experience. This book is partly a reflection on what we have experienced, with a view to coming to some worthwhile conclusions. With reflection goes analysis. Putting things into logical categories, realizing significant relationships and making worthwhile decisions—all these are examples of analytical actions. They depend not only on memory, but also on judgments about what we remember, and sometimes on moral beliefs or assumptions. As persons, reflection and analysis are essential to us.

Identity and personality

Criticism also arises from reflection, because we can compare experiences with each other, and decide why we prefer one of them.

My delightful brain-damaged godson recently went through rather a sexist phase. When his mother, to whom he had responded well all his life, did some of her usual care tasks for him, he grumbled. This is the only word which can describe his behavior. He growled when his mother said it was time to get up or have a bath. Yet when I went out to see him in his specially-adapted car when his father called round, he was laughing and responding in the happiest way. His father said that he was acting up to the men and complaining to the women.

This behavior, despite the surliness, is analytical. It depends on some conclusions about the difference between men and women. I don't for a minute think that he was sexist in the normal sense of the word. But in his very limited experience, he clearly made some decision based on gender difference and acted according to it. He changed his mind later, but I don't think he would understand about "political correctness" if you tried to explain it to him!

Bewildering world of classification

We are used to classification in every sphere of life. Language, science, music, literature, art—every type of experience involves something which can be classified. Our speech, in order to have meaning, contains different types of word—verbs, nouns, adjectives and so on. In order to travel, we carry various classifications in our mind to relate to trains, driving cars, and going in boats and aircraft. Classifications are a form of order and our lives are governed by order even if we sometimes rebel against it.

The best classifications arise out of *what is*, rather than human decisions about it. Many human classifications have to be altered because we have made mistakes or because our experience is not wide enough. In the field of medical microbiology, every so often, there is an upheaval because we did not appreciate some subtle bacteriological behavior which differed in organisms which were thought to be the same. So new species are recognized.

In the best sense, classification is a recognition of order which already exists. Human beings like to understand, and so they develop frameworks which correspond to reality as they perceive it. This is a characteristic of personality. It adds stability to our universe if we can see the relationships around us. Man is a classifying animal.

The desire for perfection

Human beings are often dissatisfied with what they encounter. When guests complained to hotel owner Basil Fawlty in the very successful television series *Fawlty Towers*, he would often complain back. And even when a comedy is not the situation, we want things to be better than they are. This is a very basic human characteristic. It is often the root of ambition, and can account for wars and other human actions.

Somehow everyone knows that everything is not perfect. Everyday suffering, crime and other tragedies tell us very loudly that imperfection is a big force in the world. Consequently, we often try to improve matters. We seek to do good, to help other people, and to make the world a better place. Even if we get things wrong and make it worse, our intention or motive is frequently to *improve* things.

The desire for perfection is present at every level of normal human life. Only those who suffer from depression or similar illnesses may show antipathy to their future. If you find no pleasure in anything, and take no steps to achieve pleasure, there is plainly something wrong in your life. But even those who possess the most expensive of everything may want more or better possessions, or surroundings. Contentment may equally well be possible whilst making attempts to improve life. You do not have to be discontented to want to put things right! I can enjoy myself reading on the train when it is delayed, but I would still like train services to be punctual.

Expressing

All persons have the ability to express themselves. The whole range of human activities perhaps cannot be listed! Human beings may be creative both scientifically and artistically, and they are often able to take something and develop it further. To be creative means to make or do something new and original; to develop may also be creative, but essentially it builds. Furthermore, human beings express themselves in a multitude of communicating activities.

There may be creativity in the lowliest of tasks. In 1971, the perceptive British businessman and politician Wilfred Brown wrote about a lift operator in a large building, whose assigned task in those days was very simple.[1] However, this man had added to his task the role of asking his passengers

---

1. Brown, *Organization*, 38.

Identity and personality

where they wanted to go on arrival at their requested floor. He would then tell them the quickest way of reaching their destination. People seek ways of expressing themselves. Personality is much more than a machine.

I am everything on the list plus . . .

It is quite impossible to give an exhaustive definition of a person. Some years ago at a conference, I sat at breakfast next to a professor who said he knew what every person needed to be happy. When I asked him what that was, he said, "Health, education and capital." I thought for a moment and said, "I think you're wrong. Everyone needs to be loved."

I can only assume that the professor in question had not reflected on his own needs. It is not the case that all you need is love, as the Beatles' song has it, but without it you may have severe problems. People who are not loved as children often grow up to be criminals, and people who are not loved as adults may become very unpleasant as a result. Love of course is an emotion, and so are hate, anger, and a whole host of other things. We are creatures of intellect and emotion, and any view of personality which neglects this is inadequate.

In passing, as I have already mentioned, there is one further huge problem about human identity for those people who think that everything is an accident, a chance occurrence. How can an accidental assembly of a large number of complex molecules come to *think* of itself as an individual person? Personally, I do not have enough faith to accept this weird belief!

I have tried to trace a few of the main factors in human personality and the list is necessarily incomplete. But a view which omits the factors I have listed is seriously deficient. Persons are complicated with many facets to their lives. We need now to consider the important phenomenon of communication, which is central to much human activity, and which comes to us from many sources.

13

Communications?

Communication and information point outside the universe

COMMUNICATION IS A TRANSMISSION of information. Marshall McLuhan, the famous professor of communication at Toronto, once described an electric light as "pure information." Light illuminates, and our eyes perceive the result. We receive information in all the ways which our senses permit, and have a wealth of communication possibilities.

Sound is another important medium of communication, because we can hear. Touch (and physical feeling) also plays a part in our most intimate communications, when we show affection, love, and sometimes anger. Smell is another medium, which may affect us both consciously, or unconsciously, as when pheromones from one person arouse sexual interest in one of the other gender.

We are told that over 90 percent of human communication is non-verbal. That is, we depend heavily on information from sources other than words and the propositions they encompass. But non-verbal communication can be misunderstood. Words can be used to clarify meaning far beyond a sigh or a dirty look. This is because words can convey precise information.

Communication and information

There is a simple rule about the relationship of communication and information. The more you have of one, the less room there is for the other. If we want to communicate most effectively, we involve the whole person and use illustrations and examples of what we are trying to say. Television is a very effective communication medium. But it carries little information. The message may be well communicated, but it needs to be short.

An example of less effective communication is the book. Even a modest book contains a great deal of information. Read a book once, and you will not remember everything. Read it again, and you will notice things which you did not first time round. But the advantage of the book is precisely the large amount of information it can contain, and to which you can return if you wish.

Communication and nature

There are many avenues of communication. Natural historians like Sir David Attenborough have chronicled many diverse ways in which plants, animals and human beings communicate with each other. Communication occurs across divides. Even the inanimate may be said to communicate, as for instance when we burn ourselves on something hot. The burn is a warning to let go quickly, and our nerves are attuned to such communications.

Sometimes there is a problem of interpretation in a communication. Deception is used to set traps by animals and human beings alike. The various species of angler fish have an attractive lure waving in front of their mouths, and when a small fish approaches this communication too close, the trap is sprung. Of course, this is final, but when human beings deceive each other in ways that are not final, what suffers is trust.

Unity, diversity and communication

Communication is only possible and indeed essential when there is a need to transmit information from one place to another. There are many levels of communication reflecting the many levels of the universe around us, and it may occur at one level or across levels. Communication is only possible because of shared experience (of persons) or qualities. We can interpret the universe around us because it is perceptible in terms of our senses, but experiences which we do not share may hide some things from us.

For instance, some birds of prey track small animals from the air by viewing ultra-violet traces in urine, and bats navigate and hunt by means of sounds which we cannot hear. The only way we can share these communications is by using techniques to translate visual and ultrasonic effects into data which we can see or hear. A bat detector on a summer night can make us vividly aware of these tiny mammals flying around and above us.

Communication therefore occurs between diverse settings, but it requires an underlying unity between the origin and destination of the message. Both ends are involved in the medium concerned. And the message may be very precise, as when it is in human words. I am drawing attention to this characteristic of communication because some people seem to ignore it completely when it comes to possible communications from the creator of the universe.

God and words

It is sometimes assumed that if a personal God were to communicate with human beings, he would not use mere human words. There are even some Christians who have held varieties of this view, and have said in effect that God communicates through our feelings. This is certainly possible to some extent, but as pointed out above, it is also possible to misinterpret messages if they are not precise.

Furthermore, there seems to be an assumption in some quarters to the effect that God would not demean himself with human words and that they are somehow a lower form of communication. There is no reason underlying this assumption, which discounts the fact that the creator made us able to communicate and receive communications. He would therefore naturally use forms of communication which we are able to understand.

Mystical views of the universe

Some people think of the highest form of communication as a direct understanding at the level of what they call spirit. Awareness or enlightenment are among the names which have been given to such messages. When you ask about their content, you do not get a direct answer. The content is held to be incommunicable except through the experience. This concept is held by some people in a variety of religions, and is not restricted to those which are pantheistic or "paneverythingistic." (Pantheism is the belief that the whole universe is god, and carries with it the tremendous problem that not only good things, but also things we find very evil are both normal, and *intended to exist.*)

Communications?

It is perfectly true that from time to time we may have experiences which we cannot communicate in words. For me that may happen, on occasion, with music or with beauty in art or nature. Though we may not be able to communicate the experience itself, it may be describable in language by its effect on us. What I wish to draw attention to, however, is that if it has no direct contact with language, then its meaning may not necessarily be clear. Some of my experiences have directly affected my emotions. I have had uncontrollable tears in my eyes when listening to a performance of Allegri's *Miserere*, for instance. But on other occasions, I have listened to this music, inwardly moved without the tears. If you asked me what its effect was, I would simply say I was greatly moved. I could not give a *meaning* to this communication, however, even though it is possible to write out the music in question.

The distinction we must draw here is between different sorts of communication. Where it is in words, or can be fully expressed in words, it can be linked to everything else of this sort. Where a communication is inexpressible in words, it can have nothing definitive to say about the universe we live in, no matter how wonderful the experience may feel.

Language, philosophy and sociology

In the early twentieth century, philosophy tended to leave the big questions alone, and instead turned to logic and language. In one sense, this was important, because the form of a human communication determines its meaning. It is right that we should be as exact as possible when speaking to each other. However, the big questions did not go away, despite some attempts to define them out of existence. I have already mentioned positivism and its verifiability criterion. If God's existence could not be verified, it was a meaningless concept according to positivism; but as the verifiability criterion could not be verified, positivism was also meaningless.

In the later twentieth century, sociology started turning the universe on its head. Instead of asking whether God was there, certain sociologists started asking the question, "Why do some people believe in God?" and answering it in a variety of ways, mostly unflattering. For instance, one idea which was widely aired was that God was a control mechanism used by some people to dominate others. This was not new, as Marx and Engels had already viewed organized religion in this way. The fact is that in *some* times and places the idea of God *has* been used in this way. But one thing was often forgotten: interesting though this sociological view might be, it had nothing to say about the actual question of whether God was really there. In this sense, such sociological views are totally irrelevant!

Understanding and interpretation

It is interesting to consider how human beings come to formulate their views. The present book is certainly focused upon this topic. However, human views are not the same as objective reality and never can be. In the objective reality which we inhabit, there *is* a definite history which has actually occurred.

Historians may argue over *what* happened, but they have an objective reference point which at least in theory can prove them right or wrong. In recent years, his relatives sought to overturn the conviction of the "A6 murderer," Hanratty, who was hanged for this crime in the 1960s before the death penalty was abolished in Britain. They wanted DNA tests to be carried out, as these were not available at the time he was convicted. However, when the tests were performed, they proved beyond doubt that the conviction was sound.[1]

In contrast, various miscarriages of justice unearthed over the past few years illustrate the personal cost which may be involved for persons convicted of crimes they did not commit. It carries the potential for a disaster of great magnitude to suggest that human views on reality are more important than reality itself. Whilst we hope the jury comes to the correct conclusion, unfortunately this does not always happen.

Communication is certainly important. This discussion shows also that human communication may have flaws, and our understanding of what is communicated may also be flawed. What about our naïve experience? That is a communication to us, since we experience it. I have tried to argue that it is important for us to understand its message. This raises two issues for us. We need to *understand* what is being said—the *words*, if you like—and we also need to *interpret* the message correctly.

1. BBC News, "Final blow."

Naïve experience interpretation

I have tried to outline the concept of naïve experience as very basic. It is so basic that we have very little scope for rival interpretations of it. The presence of *something* calls for an origin because we have not existed as persons for ever. This is the same as saying that we had a beginning. The consequences and implications of different types of origin will be discussed in chapter 14. In chapter 9, I pointed out the complexity of the *something*, and some of the things we might deduce. This was an interpretation. In the last analysis, we must test our interpretations to see whether they are true in terms of objective reality.

However, complexity requires explaining, as well as origins. How has complexity come to exist? Was it always there? Even if we work out plausible mechanisms for the development of the universe to date, there is still a big question which I outlined in chapter 9: in some way, everything has to be written in to the simplest building blocks of the universe, whatever these may turn out to be. So is there any way in which the humble quarks, leptons and force-carrying bosons can *carry the information* necessary for the existence of the most complex things we know, namely human beings? The quantity of information in one working human body is simply too large to be measured. It may be far more than the entire computer memory existing on the planet at present.

In a human being, there is a mechanism so complex it defies simple definition. The bodily structure comprises a group of systems (at least: musculoskeletal, cardiovascular, respiratory, alimentary, excretory, neurological including the senses, endocrine, immunological, reproductive, genetic and developmental), each one of which is so complex that much of the detail is unknown, and as more research is done, more difficult questions are raised requiring an answer.

Complexity on complexity

We might add to this list of complexities that human beings can study the human body and human behavior. Human beings can to some extent *understand their own physical and mental functioning and interpersonal behavior*. This self-knowledge is a further leap in complexity. Is it all written in the quarks, leptons and force-carrying bosons? Such "particles" are extremely small objects, as physicists understand them, and may not carry much in the way of information. Furthermore, some physicists think that these tiny particles are perhaps made up of even simpler particles, such as two-dimensional "branes" and one-dimensional "strings," although there is at present no experimental evidence to prove their existence.

We reach the point, therefore, where our experience is inexplicable, and the more we know about the tiny building-blocks of matter-energy, the less can be explained about why they are able to be built up into complexities like human beings. Where did the information come from to make me? The simple answer is that it was written on my genetic code. But this answer is ultimately no answer. Somehow the quarks, leptons and force-carrying bosons had to be put into the right physical configuration, and to do this, they had to carry the information in some form or other, *and in addition it had to be possible for them to do this*. It seems to me that there may be a possible answer if the information did not originate in these tiny particles—in other words, if it came from an outside source. This is one of the numerous aspects of naïve experience which points me in the direction of a creator for the universe I experience.

The greatest complexity

In my experience, the greatest complexity is that of personality. How is it possible for a human being to have self-knowledge, to be conscious? How is a human being able to know others, to have memories, to reflect, to classify and to aim at perfection? It is certainly true that there are chemical links in the brain with the human personality, and some may be affected by medicines; but that is yet another aspect of complexity. What explanations might be given?

The only scientific explanation which is given for the development of complex biological organisms like human beings is the classic account of biological evolution by natural selection. As an explanation, this fits the paleontological record of organisms which gradually increase in complexity and has much support from other evidence, such as the way in which higher embryos develop. I personally accept that it is the best explanation of the evidence we have, as do many other Christians who have worked in scientific research.[2] But the biological evolution explanation has two components. To call one component "survival of the fittest" is an excellent description of natural selection. We can understand that a frog can survive on

2. Berry, *God and Evolution*.

Communications?

land, but a fish cannot. So far, so good. Unfortunately, the other component is *random genetic mutation*, which raises a host of problems.

It is likely that genetic mutations occur primarily in response to background irradiation, which you may remember was the likely cause of my two friends' tumors mentioned in chapter 8. We are all subject to a tiny amount of this radioactivity which comes from outer space, including the sun. How can such a genetic mutation create a change in an organism to make it "fitter" in terms of survival? Here is where the problems begin. It seems that the commonest genetic mutations by far are those which do the very opposite, which make the organism likely to die instead.

Cancers are diseases which affect mainly the very young and adults from older middle age onwards. Those in the very young may often be explained by genetic harm which they inherited. The genetic system is so complicated that there is potential for it to go wrong in at least a small minority of people at the outset of their lives. But there is a large period from about 1 year to 45 years of age when cancers occur very rarely. After this, they come increasingly frequently. Why is this? One reason is that during life we gradually accumulate errors in the biological structure of our bodies. When a certain number of genetic defects has accumulated, a cancer may result.

So why should some genetic mutations be beneficial? How might they help us to survive better? The experimental evidence at present seems to say they do not, and are far more likely to harm us. While natural selection is well established, and indeed seems only to be common sense, random genetic mutation is unlikely to be beneficial, and more likely to kill. Perhaps we might say that we have reached a plateau in this mechanism, that human beings as very sophisticated organisms are unlikely to benefit further from random mutations. There is still a problem, though, with how this two-edged sword managed to help us to develop from the very earliest life-forms known.

The information problem

Thus it seems that great complexity, particularly that of the personality, poses a great question which has little chance of an answer from within the universe. The many levels of diversity, which are yet linked in the unity we perceive, are unlikely to be fully accounted for by the process of biological evolution, and even less likely to be accounted for by the initial cosmic singularity of the big bang. We may call this an *information problem*, and as we have seen, information relates to communication. Both of these together are built into our naïve experience as unity-with-diversity, which is part of the basic something-which-is-there. But does not an information problem imply that there is also a communication problem?

Indeed it does. And one of the difficulties about a question mark over communication is that it raises problems in the area of meaning. We expect the communication of information to have some meaning, otherwise it is a pointless event. But if we follow the information up, using every channel of communication open to us, and eventually come to a blank wall beyond which we cannot pass, we may rightly ask what is the use of this futility?

Communication and meaning

We experience something rather than nothing. Order, also, even the complex order of unity and diversity, the sequence of causally related events, and the fascinating role of being a participant, a self which is both distinct and separate from everything else though also linked to everything else by our physical, chemical and biological nature—all of these are a part of our experience. But this rich tapestry of life is without meaning.

I am reminded of the "atheist creed" which a schoolmaster quoted to my class several years before I became a Christian:

> There is no god; there is no devil.
> There is no heaven; there is no hell.
> I shall die like a dog, and I don't care.

Communication implies that there is meaning. It *conveys* meaning, because it contains information. When we read the daily newspaper, we are looking for meaning all the time in the events which are recorded. For there to be no ultimate meaning for *everything* paradoxically does convey a perverse meaning. It means that the many lesser levels of meaning have no meaning. What happens doesn't matter. As we saw early on, this makes all human behavior a matter of preference, not of right and wrong, because ethical concepts have no meaning. To quote a cry made famous in another context, "Who will rescue me from this body of death?"[3]

---

3. Rom 7:24b.

Might is right?

It is only when we realize the full implications of life in a limited universe—one which is unbounded yet finite—with no contact beyond, that we can grasp the horrible futility of our existence and the brute force which is pressing in all around. The endpoint of this worldview is simple to state. Might is always right. The gentle, the humble and the kind are doomed to be overrun by the violent, the arrogant and the cruel.

Perhaps some will resist this scenario, but there are no societies which last for ever. We work to protect ourselves from nuclear or biological attack by rogue states and terrorists outside, but within our society there are many who sense the futility and as a result throw off the restraints. The more who feel this way, the more our society experiences the viciousness of unbridled, unprincipled selfishness. Can criminals be controlled? Perhaps, in a police state. Is there any alternative? Yes, but if the universe holds no answer, we are compelled to look outside. What should we be looking for, and how should we seek it?

Perhaps some will try to resist this conclusion as well, because they do not want to seek an outside influence. It is noticeable however, that some atheists are attracted to the multiverse idea—the concept that there are many universes, and ours "just happens" to be one which works. They believe that there are other universes, perhaps connected with ours, and perhaps not, but they do this without a shred of evidence that these other universes exist. They reach this belief because of the many "coincidences" which make it possible for human beings on planet earth to be what they are, and for everything else on this planet and in this universe to actually exist. But the multiverse idea is intended to make our origin something which is *impersonal*, and as we shall see in chapter 14, this has dire consequences for us.

PART C

From fingerprints to identification

WE HAVE FOUND SOME fingerprints, but now they need to be linked to the person who made them. With this in mind, we shall discuss our origins, possible human explanations of reality from unbelief onwards, the matter of self-revelation by a greater person to us as persons, and the immense question of human morals.

I hope that my overall *method* of argument may be found helpful by readers. Indeed, some who follow the method will certainly be able to take the arguments further.

I am sorry if some find my arguments complicated, but equally there are others who may find them too simple. However, what I hope to do is to argue real truths, without trying to give *exhaustive* truth, which is of course impossible for finite human beings.

We shall examine the questions of where we ultimately came from, what are the possible options to account for our naïve experience, and how we can look "outside" the universe by following the clues we are given "inside" it. I shall outline indications that Christianity is what we are led to. Then we shall look at the consequences of following this path in terms of what is true and how we should behave.

14

Origins

Our experience argues for a super-personal creator

AT THIS POINT, WE are ready to consider where we came from. As stated earlier, in one sense, there are surprisingly few possibilities. They were suggested in 1972 by Francis Schaeffer, a Christian thinker, to be three, with the option of a totally meaningless existence (in which, he stated, no one could live in practice) as a fourth.[1]

Schaeffer's three options were: (1) everything came from nothing, where nothing means totally nothing, not a something like empty space—ultimately, this view means there was absolutely nothing, and then miraculously something happened to arrive on the non-existent scene; (2) everything came from something which is impersonal, and everything which exists now has always existed in some form; and (3) everything came from something personal and uncreated, which implies that the impersonal and the finite persons like ourselves are created by the greater personal origin of everything. The third view also means that the personal uncreated origin has the option of communicating with the finite created persons.

The first option Schaeffer did not think anyone had ever argued for, because it was totally against human experience. In short, while we may state the option rationally, it appears absurd in terms of our actual experience. The second includes a possible view which he called "paneverythingism," the view commonly referred to as pantheism; he pointed out that the word "pantheism" implied a personality for which there was really no evidence. It also might include the view (which Schaeffer did not mention

---

1. Schaeffer, *He is There*, 15–29.

as such) that everything is impersonal and personality as we experience it is just an accident: this view suggests that personality at least is meaningless, and with its death, morals are meaningless since everything is determined by impersonal brute forces.

The third view was argued by Schaeffer as the only possible option which made sense in the universe we experience. I hold the same view, but I would like to approach it from a slightly different direction. We live in a universe which is widely perceived as finite—that is, limited—and therefore some people have expressed the view that this finite origin is all that we can know. Some of them believe it to be impersonal and some believe it to be personal.

We come from something which is either infinite or finite. And we come from something which is either personal or impersonal. That gives four possible combinations: finite-impersonal, finite-personal, infinite-impersonal, or infinite-personal.

Finite-impersonal origin

The difficulty with any finite origin is that it automatically begs the question as to why the finite is finite. Finite means limited. Why is it limited? What limits it? If there is something which controls the finite origin in any way, it cannot be an ultimate origin. Yet the universe, according to all that is known about it, is finite. Finite, but unbounded, like the surface of a sphere, but in more dimensions, and almost inconceivably vast to us. Suppose this universe is all that exists. What are the implications for us?

First, we are stuck with Leibnitz's question. There is no answer to the question, "Why is there something, rather than nothing?" At first sight this may seem somewhat unsatisfying, but as we go further, this option becomes positively alarming. If the universe is all that exists, then there is a horrific implication in the realm of human behavior. The universe had a beginning and there are several possible endings. In the brute fact of existence, we are here, there are no rules except that we will die, and there is no meaning to human history. Ethics are dead, and preference rules instead in the realm of morals.

Our preference may be for kindness and goodness. Perhaps most of us prefer this. But it is an arbitrary choice in a finite and doomed universe. There is literally no basis for it outside preference. Laws become a matter of preference. Those who prefer cruelty and evil have just as valid a preference.

On this basis, no one could say to Hitler that he was wrong, since it is all a matter of preference. And even if more prefer what we understand as "good," they may not be able to enforce it. Ultimately, Hitler was defeated only because he had less power than his opponents did. Future "Hitlers" may not suffer the same shortcoming.

If you think that the finite, unbounded universe can somehow give us a basis for desirable human behavior, think again. It means there are no universal rules for human behavior, no rules of any kind beyond personal preference; and furthermore, human beings disagree. There are some optimists who think we may come to some agreement, but history continually proves them wrong. Some ancient cultures worshiped the sun, which was the largest source of energy they knew, and without which their crops would fail. But it gave them no basis for kindness, and some were very cruel. The Aztecs in Central America used constant human sacrifice in their religion as a way of feeding the sun.

Cruelty continues today. In the last two decades of the twentieth century and the dawn of the new millennium, for instance, no sooner has the threat of communist enslavement of the world diminished than we see an increase in hate-frenzied terrorists who are incapable of rational argument and instead carry out grotesque atrocities. From the Omagh bombing in Northern Ireland to the attack on the World Trade Center in New York, these acts show a lot of hate, but are totally lacking in any form of reason. Remember the Chinese proverb I mentioned before: he who resorts to violence thereby admits that he has lost the argument!

Even if they do not hold the finite-impersonal view themselves, such people demonstrate the problem of holding such a view. If the universe is finite and impersonal, there is no constraint on human behavior other than greater power. So much for the finite-impersonal. But there are three other options to consider.

Finite-personal origin?

Again, we have the objection that the finite is limited, and the implied question of what stands behind it and controls it, thereby preventing it from being an ultimate origin. But let's give it a chance. What could a finite-personal origin mean?

The best examples of the finite-personal origin are to be found in ancient cultures, such as the Greek gods who lived on Olympus, or the

Babylonian creation legend. Here we have gods like invincible human beings who live out their immortal existence against a backdrop of some reality which is also apparently permanent and indestructible. The question here is which came first—was it the gods, or was it the land where they exist? And in either case, what was the mechanism for producing one from the other? Next, we have to answer the question of our origin. Did these gods produce us from nothing? Or did they make us from material which happened to exist around them? Already, we are deep into problems.

Some will argue that this is a caricature. I mean it as an illustration only. That there have been cultures which seriously believed in the existence of such gods is beyond dispute. They were perhaps driven to it by a serious consideration of their experience. In this day and age, of course, there will be more sophisticated ways of stating the same view, perhaps in terms of space travelers and time lords. However, the unrealism of the finite-personal view is borne out by there being no serious contender on the world scene today.

Yet there is one advantage to this solution. If a finite origin is a problem, a personal origin nevertheless helps us with one matter. An impersonal origin means that our personality is a mere accident, and carries no meaning to it other than that we are of greater complexity than impersonal objects around us. There can be no ethical rules, no standards for behavior other than personal preference. But a personal origin means that there can be responsibility—an obligation to the person who made us.

Infinite-impersonal origin?

So it is easy to see the problem in an infinite-impersonal origin. No personality in the origin, and we are correspondingly debased. It is all without meaning, without sense, because the impersonal is unthinking and automatic. If we are the product of that, then our thinking is an accident. The beauty of our literature, art and music, the achievements of our science and technology: all is an empty nothing because it is an accident, not *intended* to exist.

The infinite-impersonal origin is typically stated today as the multiverse view of the universe.[2] It is against the probabilities that our universe should be so complex, encompassing so many levels of order including our own personalities. So perhaps it is one of many such universes, one that happens to work.

2. Rees, *Just Six Numbers*, 166–79.

This is an interesting idea for which there is not a scrap of evidence, because we cannot get outside our own universe. So we are asked to disregard all the signals, the evidence for the origin of our universe, because there might just be lots more universes—but ones which do not work! Ours then turns out to be the one instance in which things happened to achieve greater complexity, purely by accident.

This idea of accident needs some examination. The idea is that if you have enough possible universes, then somehow one of them may be striving to achieve greater complexity. For an impersonal object, even an infinite-impersonal, this striving takes a lot of believing. Indeed it takes a faith, but not a faith for which there is some evidence. Some would call it pretty unbelievable in comparison with a faith in a personal-infinite creator! And this brings us to the one believable scenario.

Infinite-personal origin?

There are two sorts of infinite-personal origin. One is the origin which is distinct from what is produced and the other is the origin which gradually develops to form everything. The former is the creation concept, and the latter is what is generally known as pantheism. We saw above that Schaeffer considered pantheism to be illusory, but let us start from what some people seem to believe.

There is an immediate objection to pantheism—where is there any evidence of the universe having a personality? And furthermore, how could it manifest any of the characteristics of personality which we examined earlier? This is the same problem as that of the quarks, leptons and force-carrying bosons. What personality do they have? All the evidence points to the universe being impersonal but with many personalities occurring within it—ourselves. Furthermore, the universe appears to be finite, limited, and therefore an unlikely ultimate origin for all that exists. In passing, we might remember that Sir Arthur Conan Doyle wrote a short story called *When the World Screamed*. This was not some modern disaster story, but a humorous account of scientists making a hole through the earth's crust, and when they finally got through it, the planet itself screamed!

There is one further problem if the universe is a giant personality in itself, a problem I have already mentioned. In the universe there are good and evil, truth and untruth, kindness and cruelty, joy and suffering. Pantheism implies that these are equally ultimate and an *essential* part of what exists. What we feel about them doesn't matter; there is ultimately no difference between them. Baudelaire is reputed to have said, "If there is a god, he is the devil." If pantheism is true, this is strictly correct.

Perhaps now we may consider the idea of a personal creator. A super-person, greater than the universe, created it, gave it shape, wrote into it all the basic physical laws which would make chemistry and life possible, including personal beings. With this separation from the universe, we can also see that the evil in the universe may not be present in the creator. With a creator kind and generous enough to give the freedoms of life to his creatures, it is possible that the evil arose from the latter. Indeed, this concept is central to Christian belief.

Nor is it out of place to consider that this super-person might have a super-personality. The arguments for one God are compelling, but the arguments for that God encompassing unity and diversity in his inmost being are even more compelling. For a super-personality to exist, he will be on a higher level than our single persons. There is only one worldview in existence which centers on such a super-person—the religion known as Christianity. The God of Christianity alone is a super-person who encompasses diversity within his own being: from his communication to us, we may know him as three persons but in one God.

The super-person

What is it that forces us to the view that a person who is God must of necessity be a super-person? First, the concept of personality itself. We saw earlier that a person manifests personality by virtue of certain characteristics. A person is not a non-person, because: a person recognizes self as distinct from non-self; a person has an identity, a memory, an ability to communicate, and an ability to create. And a God who is a creator would in some way encompass the whole of creation at the level of perfection, and far more as well! We could not begin to guess what God is unless he showed us, and unless he gave us some markers in what he has made—what might be called signposts towards him, fingerprints which he has left on the universe.

What if God were a person and not a super-person? There would be several problems. First, we would need to account for the nature of his creation. It is of the most wonderful diversity: where did this come from if God is not of an even higher quality of diversity? Did God make something which is greater than himself? At the same time, the universe constitutes a unity, a whole which includes parts. Is God less than a complete unity?

Secondly, within this universe there are many amazing wonders, but perhaps nothing which compares with the wonder of love. We rightly accord a high place to human love in this world, and the highest aspect of human love is that love *gives* to another person. The most formidable statement in the Bible is that God *is* love.[3]

Super-personality and love

How can this be true? We might say, for example, that God created the universe because he wanted to show self-giving love, which is true. But this also might imply that he is somehow incomplete in himself, that without the universe there was no way in which God could show his love. If he is the infinite-personal God of whom we are talking, he did not need the universe, and he is complete in himself. How can we imagine a God who encompasses the great power of love within his own self? Only if *within* himself there is the ability to actually love.

We begin to see how God might be a super-person. If God has made himself known to us in the Bible, it begins to make sense that he is not simply a person as we are persons, but someone on an altogether higher plane of existence, who is infinite and yet exhibits super-personality. This is why Jesus, who we are told existed before his birth and indeed before the creation, was able to talk to his followers about the Father, and proclaim himself to be the Son, and to emphasize that the Father and the Son were united in eternity.

There was yet more for the early Christians to take in. Jesus had come from eternity into human history for specific purposes, but he also left this history in a way not determined by those who put him to death, as he showed his power by overcoming death, and left at a later date. Yet Jesus promised his followers the coming of another person, who was known as the Holy Spirit. This event happened in due course, transforming the followers and spreading the church through many nations. There are also some pointers to God's super-personality in the Old Testament, the Hebrew Bible which contains prophecies of the coming of Jesus from many centuries earlier.

---

3. 1 John 4:8.

Thus God made himself known as one who is a unity but who also encompasses diversity in such a way as to manifest love within his own self. Without the need for a creation, the Father, the Son and the Holy Spirit have loved each other from all eternity, and yet God is not three, but shows himself as three-in-one. This is the point at which our understanding reaches another limit. Why God should be essentially of triune (three-in-one) personality, rather than any other possible form of super-person, is a question for which we have no answer beyond that he has made it known to us, but there is no doubt that the answer fits the universe in which we live. A super-person of infinite dimensions and power lies outside this creation, and he can directly influence any point of space-time.

We are not concerned with the *how* of these matters, but rather the question of *what* is possible for the actual universe which we experience. Many things are beyond our comprehension, but if we have no answer to the question of origins, then we have ultimately no basis for how we should behave, or even for what we can know. Our answer to this question also matters, because it helps us to determine what is true and what is good. The super-person has left his stamp on our experience in such a way that we can rule out those ideas which do not conform to his creation. Maybe we cannot prove God from his creation, but perhaps we can rule out certain ideas of God as disproven.

To conclude this chapter, there is only one origin which is fully compatible with the messages of our naïve experience. Our personalities do not have a question mark hanging over them if we originated in the will of an infinite-personal creator. And if that creator encompasses both unity and diversity, he can have the perfection of being the ultimate super-person and also the perfection of including such qualities as love within himself. No other answer can be given to the questions thrown at us by our experience unless that experience is meaningless and accidental. As we have seen, there are reasons for believing that it is not.

15

Possibilities

Naïve experience leads us to a particular type of religion and the prime contender is Christianity

WE ARE NOW REACHING the point when we can consider the principal views of religion held today by many people. There is the view that all religion is a source of conflict and unworthy of modern scientific man. Then there is the view that God is a machine which regulates everything but has no personality. There is also the view that God coincides with everything which we experience. And there is the view that God is a person or a super-person who created everything else and who takes an interest in how that "everything else" is.

"Religion is wrong"

The first observation to be made about this view is that it is not only unrealistic, but self-contradictory. What is a religion? Followers of this view sometimes say that it is belief in a god for whom there is no evidence. But to do this they disregard the first question, "Why is there anything?"

If they try to answer that question, they are forced to make what, by their own definition, are religious assertions about reality. To say that everything has always existed, for instance, is to make an assertion for which there is no evidence. In order even to act in this world, such believers in non-belief are in fact accepting the evidence of their senses, but interpreting this evidence to mean whatever they choose! They are acting in a realm of faith, while trying to say that faith is wrong!

And as we have seen, there is no evidence for atheism. To say there is no god of any sort inside or outside the universe is to move in the most extreme region of faith, a belief which can only be rational if you have total knowledge about absolutely everything. As I pointed out in chapter 1, atheism is either totally irrational, or the ultimate mysticism!

Agnosticism is a more reasonable faith. But it is still a faith. You need some beliefs in order to live. For instance, the uniformity of natural causes would help. But how can this belief be justified? Again, you can only say that it is true up to the extent you have experienced it. For the universe in general, you do not have the knowledge required to say it is universally true.

This is the incomprehensibility of atheism and agnosticism. On its face, this group of beliefs seems to be eminently reasonable. Such "non-believers" say that they want evidence for what they believe. But they omit this at the central point, namely, why should they believe anything at all? Well, what happens if you believe nothing? The answer is that you *do* nothing! There is no basis for anything at all. But you have to live, even if the world appears incomprehensible. Do you? Why do you have to live? Well, suicide is not a reasonable option. That is true! Not even suicide is reasonable—because for believers in nothing, nothing at all is reasonable!

The impossibility of non-belief

This is the impossible situation of all who try to say that they do not need a religion. They actually have one, defined by their "unbelief," whereas others have a religion defined by their belief. The most impossible situation of all is that of total unbelievers. On the face of it they believe in magic: there is nothing to believe in, yet they do believe in something in order to live. But if you try to find out what they do believe, oh what a tangled web they weave! And if we take such people to be sincere (they often appear to be extremely sincere), then it seems to me that they are sincerely mistaken. The self-contradiction in their faith is built in and impossible to eradicate.

What is this self-contradiction? Perhaps we may call it their belief in unbelief, or the idea that they will select some things which they happen to prefer in their experience, whilst rejecting others which are equally present in that experience. Before the acceptance of naïve experience, they are indulging in some reasoning which excludes part of the experience as unacceptable. On what grounds do they do this? Preference alone. There is nothing in reason or experience which can validate such behavior. If you rule out a possibility without evidence, you are not acting reasonably.

Preference and evidence

Some may object at this point that the argument may apply to atheists, but is rather hard on the agnostic. After all, the agnostic is not ruling out religious belief, but rather saying that the evidence is insufficient. Unfortunately, even the agnostic has a religion of preference, not of evidence. It seems humble enough to say, "I don't know," but this is not always what the agnostic seems to be saying. If the agnostic really believes this, then he or she should be open to anything which could replace the lack of knowledge with knowledge. Without such openness, it may be difficult to believe in the agnostic's sincerity. The lack of knowledge sometimes seems to be a determination *not* to know. I was once an agnostic, and like many other agnostics (like Francis Schaeffer, for instance) I became a Christian because I found Christianity was more reasonable. It faced up to the real universe, and especially to the fact of personality.

The preferences of an individual may be well hidden, but we all suffer from them. At best they are what are called presuppositions; you may also call them assumptions or axioms, and openly acknowledge that you have them. At worst, preferences are poor judgments founded on inadequate evidence. Between these two extremes lie many possibilities. I have tried to show in this book that our presuppositions should be as few as possible. We should let naïve experience show us the way to think about the universe, ourselves and origins.

What might be called my presuppositions? Well, certainly my desire to begin with raw naïve experience and nothing else is founded on one of my assumptions about the nature of reality. I hold the presupposition that we should avoid all other presuppositions! If you think about it, this is a way to try and avoid bias from the very outset. However, you must not forget that I am a reasoning, thinking human being and my past experience has had a lot to do with how I now approach reality. You need to consider the question, "Is there a better way?" Is it best to try to wipe out everything except the most basic experiences we have in order to reach the soundest basis for reasoning? If you agree with me, we can go further. If not, please consider how your disagreement with me may affect my subsequent argument. I would say that the more you presuppose, the more you lay yourself open to possible internal contradiction, and the more complicated is your faith-system—your religion—of belief or unbelief.

In the beginning

What does naïve experience show us? It gives us an immediate close knowledge of something against which no argument can be advanced. If you like, it is an Archimedean point. The Greek philosopher Archimedes said, "Give me a fixed point and I will move the world." From our definite, fixed naïve experience, we may understand certain very basic concepts. There is something rather than nothing. It is an ordered something, it exists in many complex levels of order, it shows sequential change, with cause and effect sometimes apparent, and it is also divisible into *me* and *everything else*.

The *me* is a definite person. I have an identity, memory, an ability to reflect and classify, and a desire for perfection. At a very basic level, the *everything else* is far from perfect, and I want to do something about it. In order to act within the everything else, we have to make decisions, and to make good decisions we have to answer questions. We cannot avoid making some decisions, even if we prefer not to think about them. The first question is how it all originated. Though physicists may argue about the details of the big bang, I need a realistic starting-point. Does *everything* begin with the big bang? If so, then everything is a total mystery. There is no explanation for my naïve experience and no implication for my behavior. I am in an amazing, mind-boggling universe which means absolutely zilch. My personality is similarly totally without meaning. So is every characteristic I associate with it: thought, love, hope—all are empty words.

As we have seen, only if the universe originated at the instigation of an outside person can it have any meaning. But we must also consider a few things about that person. Can the universe be a part of or an extension of that person? If so, we are back to de Sade. What is, is right. Good and evil are equally present *and intended* in what is. There is no difference between the cruel and the kind. We are helplessly caught up in a life which cries out for a moral code, and there can be none. There is no Law, only human laws which are contrived and sometimes arbitrary. Truly, this is a form of damnation. Such is the consequence of any pantheism or paneverythingism.

But a super-person who exists permanently and who has brought into existence a finite universe is a creator, and is separate from the universe. In this case, if the creator is specifically and positively *good*, then we must seek the origin of evil within the universe. If the creator is not good, then all the arguments apply that applied to pantheism. How do we know what is true of a creator who is "outside" the universe? There is only one way: for the creator to reveal his nature to us.

Revelation: natural and special

From our starting point of naïve experience, we have let ourselves perceive the something-which-is-there, and drawn some conclusions from it. This process might also be represented as a *revelation*, with the something-which-is-there communicating itself to us. In short, the attention we pay to naïve experience is actively to receive a revelation, a disclosure, both from our selves and also our surroundings. This may be called a *natural* form of revelation. It corresponds to observation on our part, and not to experiment, where we manipulate aspects of the reality around us and then observe the results.

Special revelation is quite specific in contrast, and needs to be communicated in human language for us to understand. At this point, we have to consider the possible options. They constitute all theistic religions—all those religions in which the god is a creator and a person. If we exclude for the moment the religions originating in the last two centuries and especially in the United States, the options are remarkably limited. The choice lies between Judaism, Christianity and Islam, in order of their historical origin.

It is interesting that these three religions are related. Christianity had its historical origin in Judaism and claims to be the fulfillment of prophecies in the Jewish Bible, which Christians call the Old Testament. Islam depends on both Judaism and Christianity, some parts of which it accepts, and some parts of which it rejects. Islam has a sacred book, the Qur'an, but in practice also accords authority to some parts of the Old and New Testaments. Muslims, like Jews, trace their lineage back to Abraham. Christians also consider Abraham to be their religious ancestor, in the sense that they believe God's promises to Abraham are made to those who, like them, follow in the faith of Abraham.

It would be an enormous task to compare these three religions, let alone all the other religions in the world, but we need to ask a question concerning them, as we have done already about the possible origin of everything. The question we now need to ask concerns the revealed nature of God in these three religions. What sort of God is at the centre of Judaism, Christianity or Islam? Here is one central point at which we may find some guidance as to which concept might be really true, for there are distinct differences which are recognized by adherents of the three religions. For instance, can we say that our naïve experience directs us to one or other religion because of the relationship between the creator and the creation?

Agreement and disagreement between religions of revelation

There is considerable agreement between the religions of written revelation—they have been called "religions of a book" on this account—on certain aspects of God. First, he is viewed as creator, and is the source of all that is good. He is a person, and in his perfection he is one God. It is also interesting that the various religions which have worshipped a multiplicity of gods—polytheistic religions—have often viewed one of these gods as above the others. Hence Zeus in ancient Greek religion, and Brahma in Hindu religion have been seen in this way. What is different in monotheistic religions is that the person of God is so unique that nothing else is comparable. He alone is self-existent, self-consistent, completely self-sufficient and perfect. There are no others possible like him.

Secondly, this self-sufficient person is the creator of all that exists. Creation was entirely voluntary, and in no way compelled, for there is nothing which can compel God. In this creation, he made human beings to share some of his experiences, though obviously in a limited way. The creation may therefore be viewed as an act of kindness or of love, and we have certain freedoms as a result.

Thirdly, because it is his, the creation is *responsible* to God. He is just and good, and gives laws for us to obey. It is precisely because we and other non-material beings have *dis*obeyed God that evil exists in his creation. The abuse of freedoms given by God causes problems in what would otherwise be total harmony. It is viewed always as *sin*, a crime first and foremost against God, and only secondarily against other human beings.

In what ways do revealed religions differ?

The three religions therefore agree that God is one person, that he is the creator and the giver of laws for us to obey. In what prime ways do they differ? We might say first that both Judaism and Islam place a great emphasis on the place of God's law in human life. The Jews of Jesus' time had great pride that their nation had been entrusted with God's law. Good deeds also have a very important place in the practice of Islam. Because people do wrong so often, they have to try to compensate for their failure by obedience, and if possible, by acts of merit. Only thus can they hope to receive forgiveness when they stand before God for his judgment.

Christianity claims both to include and supersede Judaism. The Hebrew Bible (the Christian Old Testament) contains remarkable prophecies of a Messiah or Christ. Both these words refer to a person anointed (the practice of anointing with oil denotes a king) by God, who would appear in human history at God's appointed time to achieve a tremendous work of saving God's people. At the time of Jesus, however, many Jews looked for a political salvation from their Roman overlords, but those who became Christians realized that salvation meant something far greater—salvation from the just punishment by God of sins of all types, and also a renewed freedom to obey God and avoid sin to a significant extent.

God as revealed through Jesus Christ

Quite clearly, Christianity takes its name from Jesus Christ, and its emphasis on him is considerable. He is seen as the son both of God and of a representative human being. Because he is God, he existed before the creation. He also became man and came as God's greatest self-revelation to human beings. But because he is God, he is without sin, unlike any other human being. He was therefore perfect as man, also, and because of this perfection, His death was a unique sacrifice, a payment of the penalty for sin which no one else could render.

Because Jesus claimed so clearly to be God—for instance, using God's personal name of himself; claiming to do things which only God could do; working stupendous and well-attested miracles with the authority and power he had as Creator—the early Christians had a difficulty. Was Jesus exactly the same as the person he addressed as the Father? And who was the Holy Spirit? In the Hebrew Bible, the Holy Spirit was mentioned in a way which indicated he was God's "breath," bringing life. But Jesus referred to the Holy Spirit as a separate person who could act in real human history.

When he departed from earth, as recorded at the end of the Gospel of Matthew, Jesus told his followers to help people of every nation to become followers like themselves. He added a very significant statement. He told his followers to baptize (a sign of Christian initiation, a symbol of being washed clean) the new followers or disciples in the *name* of the Father, *and* of the Son, *and* of the Holy Spirit: *not*, you will note, in the *names* of these three persons, but in the single *name*. The statement clearly shows that Jesus knew himself to be God the Son, and the Holy Spirit to be a person. This is just one of many clear statements in the New Testament of the Christian Bible showing that these three persons are one God, one super-person.

Jesus himself was fully aware of the importance of being precise. In another place in the New Testament, he made it very clear that the Jewish patriarchs, the founders of the Jewish people, though they had long since died, were yet alive with God. He confounded some Jews (Sadducees) who did not believe that the body could be raised from the dead, by showing that God in his own words had described himself as relating to these patriarchs in the present, not simply in the past.[1]

The Holy Trinity: a description which solves problems

The resolution of the questions raised by the words of Jesus was easy to state, but difficult to visualize. The Christians knew that there is only one God, and their writings in the New Testament emphasize this. But they saw that Jesus had revealed to them a complexity within God which could only be explained by three-persons-within-one. Thus God was seen as triune (tri-une) and the whole person of God was described as the Holy Trinity of Father, Son and Holy Spirit. If we accept this Christian description, three significant difficulties about God immediately disappear.

The first difficulty is how God can be totally self-sufficient without having to create anything, when there is apparently no one else for him to relate to. How could the tremendous quality of self-giving love exist if there is only one person in existence? How could God's love be there to such an extent that he is actually described in the New Testament as *being* love?[2] The Christian understanding of God removes this difficulty. Before all creation, the Father, Son and Holy Spirit communed in love with each other within the Godhead.

The second difficulty is how God relates to a creation which contains unity and diversity as a basic characteristic. The Holy Trinity embodies this characteristic: there are three persons in one God. What we experience in the universe as basic is present in the very Person of God. God is greater than his creation and contains *in himself* all its good characteristics.

And thirdly, what does it mean to be a person, to have a distinct self? How can God be a person and completely perfect if there is no way for him to manifest personality without creating persons? How could he exist as a person before creation? Again, the revelation of Jesus Christ is that God is,

---

1. Matt 22:23–33.
2. 1 John 4:8b.

always has been, and always will be a super-person, and that he embodies more than one personality.

Opinions of other religions on Christianity

We will consider briefly the views held by adherents of major and minor religions on the person of Jesus Christ and the Holy Trinity. In Judaism, Jesus is not thought of as the Christ, who is presumably yet to come; the difficulty is that he fulfils all the prophecies so well. Muslims believe that Jesus was a prophet, but that he was not allowed to die on the cross; this is in stark contrast to the Christian view that Jesus accomplished something no one else could do by dying there. In other world religions the views vary; some Hindus, for instance, will honor Jesus as god, but for them he is simply another god alongside the other Hindu deities.

If we look briefly at the many minor religions which have started mainly in the USA since the middle of the nineteenth century, to my knowledge not one of them accepts that God is a Holy Trinity. Jehovah's Witnesses have their own special version of the Bible in which they have tried to obliterate the many references to Jesus as God. Jehovah's Witnesses also corrupt Greek texts showing the Holy Spirit is God. The Jehovah's Witness version of the Bible also mistranslates as "it" the pronoun (he) referring to the Holy Spirit which occurs several times in John 14–16. In the original Greek, this pronoun in each instance is given in the masculine gender—he—although the word for Spirit is neuter in gender, as an impersonal thing would be. This is a clear indication of the personality of the Holy Spirit. The Mormons add three other books to the Bible and reject its teaching on these matters. Numerous other minor religions or cults act similarly in denying that Jesus is the Christ, the person of God born as man, and that God is triune.

In all religions where these two concepts are denied, there tends to be a similar emphasis on good deeds to put the individual right with God, since Jesus as mere man could not do this. There is also a clear problem over the three difficulties outlined in the last section: if God is not a super-person who is complex at the level of personality, it is really difficult to see how he relates to his creation.

It is worth noting the similarities between many religions on the question of good works, and the remarkable difference in Christianity. In religions other than Christianity, the good works are supposed to be something you do in order to achieve your own salvation, but the real problem is how this can be done. Is it really possible to balance your evil deeds with good, or is there a sense in which the evil is a permanent and damning stain on your life? In Christianity, by contrast, you are saved by Jesus dying on the cross and removing the evil from you if you are willing to change your life, so that you are *then* able to do good works. This is not automatic; you are involved in a far-reaching change of life, beginning a permanent relationship with God, and actively bringing the whole of your life into tune with his rules.

Conclusion: Christianity fits and Christianity works

In a short chapter it is not possible to discuss all the religions of the world. We have looked at the essential matters concerning the nature of God in order to see how the Christian view fits the universe we live in. There are many other matters which might be discussed, but without a clear understanding of how our experience in the universe is related to the creator of all, we may well go astray. Of course, we may reject the idea of this three-in-one loving creator, but we do so at our peril. Rejecting him does not only imply problems when we face him on the judgment day. It carries clear implications for human society and each one of us now. Rejecting the real God is the same as accepting hell.

In a previous chapter, we discussed the matter of experience, and specifically of testing our rationally formed ideas. Ideas need testing, and none more so than those of religion. It is interesting that Islam apparently does not permit the investigation of the Qur'an or any questioning of Mohammed's claims. In the strict practice of Islam, such acts apparently carry the death penalty. What this means is that there is no way in which evidence for the possible truth of Islam may be discussed, since it would include discussing the possible *un*truth of Islam as well. On the other hand, Christianity views *all* truth as God's truth, and you are positively welcomed to investigate whether the Bible is reliable, and whether Jesus truly lived and died and rose from the dead.

If Christianity is true, a lot of things follow. The God who made us is also interested in each and every one of us. He wants us freely to relate to him, and enjoy his company in our lives, and after our deaths. Jesus died but he also rose again from the dead, and now he invites us to follow him. Jesus said that he had come so that we might have the fullest sort of life.[3]

3. John 10:10.

Possibilities

    The marvel is not so much that God *can* do these things, as that he *does* do them. It stretches the mind to think that the God who created the entire universe also shows his love to billions of individual people to whom he sends messages. These messages are partly through his creation, which may guide us towards him, but also much more specifically in the Christian Bible. Real Christianity is a continual experiment, relying upon the God who has spoken to us, trying to obey him and experiencing his wonderful love for us.

16

Purity and profanity

Morals depend on something real outside the universe

AT THE END OF Disney's film of *Fantasia* there come two tremendous spectacles: profanity is represented by Moussorgsky's *Night on a Bare Mountain* with damned persons dancing in the hand of a monstrous devil or demon, and then purity is given its moment in a milder and definitely benign visual setting of Schubert's *Ave Maria*.

I don't know what you think, but for me the profanity has a definitely greater impact. There is something exciting about the forces of evil, though Moussorgsky and Disney definitely limited them to the hours of darkness, which is not present in the purity of the lovely music of the *Ave Maria*.

Too often it seems that excitement is limited to evil. Only the truly bad can truly excite us. People like exciting novels and especially films about tremendous crimes. Or maybe it's tragedy which we find far more exciting than comedy. How close the two are is shown in some modern versions of Shakespeare. I have two videos of *Twelfth Night* and one is not so much hilarious comedy as a tragic black comedy in which Malvolio is very unjustly cruelly hurt.

The point is further illustrated by Tolkien's epic saga, *Lord of the Rings*. In the 2001 film version of the first part, one of the most exciting good characters, Tom Bombadil, was omitted completely! Perhaps it was thought that the audience would find it a little tiring to see someone who was just good with no other redeeming features! Obviously a long story may be reduced in length for a film, but why omit this character? Who knows, perhaps the film-makers knew more about their audiences than we suspect?

Purity and profanity

Why is purity so boring?

To be fair to creative artists like film-makers, purity often wins. But sometimes it seems to be a warped version of purity. In films like *Fatal Attraction*, the hero is far from pure and more likely to be a victim through making some moral mistake. The only people who are viewable as "innocent" tend to be further from the centre of action.

Part of the problem of purity is that it seems so unbelievable. In an age when many teenagers have lost their virginity before the age of consent, the idea of remaining a virgin until you marry the person you have courted as Mr. or Miss Desirable is almost unbelievable to some. There is also a tendency to describe earlier generations as hypocrites who did not practice the chastity they preached. And some high profile people who are caught out in their waywardness are occasionally viewed sympathetically as though they are victims of a muckraking press.

What can we say of excitement from the good? Well, many find excitement in sciences, the spectacles of astronomy and particle physics, the beauties of natural history and the fascination of chemistry. But this is often the excitement of predictability, although science is not without its surprises and beauties. We are fascinated by the unpredictable, and for that we may need human involvement. And where there is human involvement, there is always the question of morals. Often in art and literature, and occasionally in music, morals are to the fore.

What of those who seek purity?

Although it does not appear so exciting, there have been many who sought purity. Many thousands have entered a monastic life to rid themselves of the foulness which they so often encountered. The Pharisees at the time of Jesus were proud of the Law with which God had entrusted them, and went to great lengths to keep it to the letter. Indeed, this was one reason why Jesus found fault with them. He accused them of keeping the Law in such a way as to avoid their obligations to others. In short, he accused them of lacking love, and of rewriting the Law in ways God never intended.

There are so many religions in which you are supposed to achieve salvation, enlightenment or some other goal by *doing* things. Even Christianity degenerated to this corrupt form in the Middle Ages. In 1533 Martin Luther recounted, "I was indeed a pious monk and kept the rules of my order so strictly that I can say: If ever a monk gained heaven through monkery, it should have been I. All my monastic brethren who knew me will testify to this."[1] And in the twenty-first century, it is no different. New religions from the last hundred years or so of human history are all out there saying you have to try harder, you have to do better, you have to follow this or that way of salvation. You *ought* to live this way, to make the world a better place. There are at least two problems in this type of reasoning.

How do we go from "is" to "ought"?

First, to say that something *is* the case is factual only. It has no moral weight whatever. Yet people have tried to build moral structures on compelling biological evidence, making use of our unseen motives and feelings such as pity and compassion. David Attenborough, who is a thoughtful humanist, made a strong case for good ecological behavior by human beings in his *State of the Planet* television series. The planet is beautiful and we are spoiling it. Biodiversity is something we all enjoy and benefit from. Other campaigners have made similar points. But how strong is this argument? After all, species have died in the past; *should* we even try to preserve those which are naturally selected for extinction? Might this not risk other sorts of ecological disaster? After all, we are just a part of nature. The moral argument therefore is not clear: *is* does not mean *ought*. Personally, I accept the argument, but that is because I am a Christian, and because I know Christians should look after God's wonderful creation.

Secondly, facts may be argued about. Take, for example, global warming. Thirty years ago, some researchers worried about global *cooling*. This was not academic: the last ice age, during which the northern part of the British Isles was covered, ended about 12,000 years ago. Weather is not static. The temperature ripples up and down, and there are both short-term and long-term ripples. It is difficult to understand fully what is changing at present.[2]

Then we need to know about the factors which determine our climate. The most important appears to be the sun, and the sun also varies from time to time, for instance, in sunspot activity, which affects our climate. Uncertainty about its effects leads to greater uncertainty about the effects of human activities. Uncertainty is a bad basis for morality. Do we need to cool or warm the earth? Do we want to flood Britain, or cover it with ice?

1. Hillerbrand, *Reformation in its own Words*, 24.
2. Esper, "Cooling trend."

Purity and profanity

Again, as a Christian, I know we should try not to damage God's beautiful earth, but I want to be certain *how* to protect it.

The problem is that facts are no basis for morals

But whatever the *facts*, there is no clear link between arguments on either side of the environmental divide and what we *should* do. Our actions presuppose *motives*. Facts have no moral impetus of their own. If I were still an agnostic, I could say that since our world is doomed, what does it matter what we do, so long as we enjoy ourselves? Why should we do anything about it? Some years ago, a program televising court proceedings from Florida riveted my attention. The jury had to decide whether a convicted criminal should receive the death penalty for a murder. The District Attorney was in favor of this, and he said, "Ladies and gentlemen of the jury, why should you and I pay our taxes in order to keep this worthless person alive?"

To some people, this might seem a good argument for executing a murderer. But it wholly misses the moral point. The question to be answered is whether the person concerned *deserves* to be executed. If justice is to be the business of the courts, the personal interest of those making the decision is irrelevant. Furthermore, the question assumed something wholly unprovable, namely whether anyone can be valued as totally worthless. Jesus asked God the Father to forgive those who crucified him; he did not view them as worthless.

Just to put a strong case *against* the death penalty, the famous Russian writer Fyodor Dostoevsky (1821-1881), a Christian, was sentenced to death for alleged political crimes in 1849 and reprieved at the last minute. He later wrote a passionate argument to say the death penalty was never justifiable.[3] Why? Because until life was extinguished, even the murderer's victim had at least some hope of living. Dostoevsky argued that the death penalty was always *unjust* because it was out of proportion even to the crime of murder, by substituting the *certainty* of death.

How do we go from facts to morals? The answer is that we cannot. But there is a much deeper problem about good and evil which affects all of us. Is it even possible to be good? The question of purity is tied up with how difficult we ourselves find it to be pure. Can any of us say we are pure? Many of the kindest, gentlest, most loving people are also acutely aware of

---

3. Dostoevsky, *Idiot,* chapter 2.

their own shortcomings. How can we relate to that which is totally without impurity? God is separated from us by an unimaginable gulf.

The problem of being good

How good are you? How good am I? We tend to answer this sort of question by comparing ourselves with others. A long-established burglar was once accused of picking pockets, and he was most indignant. "Yes, I know I've broken into large houses and taken valuable things there," he said, "but picking pockets is plainly immoral. You might be taking the only belongings the person had. You might be forcing his children to starve. I wouldn't ever do that." Likewise, there is often a form of satisfaction for people in finding that someone else has done something far worse than they would ever dream of. So where do you draw the line?

When I was about 12 years of age, I stole a small item of confectionery from a shop. It is the only thing I can ever recall stealing. No one ever found out. Four years later I became a Christian. I'll tell you more about that later. But this one act then came back to haunt me. I went back to the shop to own up and put things right, but it was no longer there. What made it far worse was that the shopkeeper had been a very kindly man and I felt really bad about what I had done. *But there was no way I could put it right.* In a very simple way, I learned the meaning of the conscience which I had previously suppressed.

How might I rationalize what I had done? I might say that children often do things out of daring, and that it was not really wrong, only a child's attempt to have an adventure. But one thing I had learned was that stealing was wrong. It hurt me far more to think I had hurt someone who was a pleasant, kind person. What if he had been the opposite? Well then, the chances are I wouldn't have risked the possibility of being caught! It was because of his kindness, paradoxically, that I had stolen from him. Such is the perversity of our behavior!

So how did my theft compare with other people's misdeeds? I cannot compare it with them. I do not know the actual effects of my theft. If I had been reassured by the shopkeeper that it was of little significance, that might have helped me to feel better about it. But time had moved on, and I had no way of knowing its consequences. Therefore there is no way I can compare the deed with others.

Purity and profanity

Where do we draw the line?

Breaking the law varies from minor offences to major villainy. Many people break traffic laws, which they regard lightly, but as a consequence, some innocent people are hurt. Fewer deliberately commit crimes like robbery, rape, child abuse and murder—all of which will hurt innocent people.

Most people have no convictions for anything. Are they therefore better than those who have been caught? Not necessarily. The week I wrote this, DNA evidence undeniably linked a man who died of cancer a few years ago with the brutal deaths of three girls some years previously. How many of us are secretly criminals?

The truth is that purity is a matter of our inmost being, and none of us is likely to be clean there. Jesus made it clear that the secret desire to do something wrong, like murder or adultery, was as bad in one sense as the act itself. Why? Because purity is a matter of what we are like. Of course, to commit murder or adultery is to hurt someone else. But to want to hurt someone is to damage ourselves. And when God looks at us, he does not think only about the consequences of what we have done because, as with my theft, we may have no control over them. God's view is of our innermost nature, and therein lies the problem. How can we claim purity when our minds entertain ideas which are anything but pure?

It was this problem which afflicted people like Martin Luther. Trying to do good in our ineffective way does not in any way undo our evil. Time moves on and the evil is fixed, a part of the past which can no longer change. What are the alternatives? We may recognize the evil, deny it, or hide it.

These alternatives are equally useless to us. Recognition of our misdeeds does not put things right. Denial, which seems very prevalent today, is living a lie which others may know to be a lie. And to hide our evil deeds is to fool others but not ourselves. According to Solzhenitsyn in his novel *The First Circle*, even Stalin was tormented by conscience, which accounts for why he protected and welcomed certain religious officials.

How far removed from us is purity?

The prophet Isaiah, in the Old Testament, pictures our good deeds as nothing more than filthy rags patched together over us.[4] Why filthy rags? Because it shows the difference between us and God. At our very best, we are

---

4. Isa 64:5.

dirty and almost naked before him. Could you get into the presence of the Queen or the President in such a state? Definitely not! So why do we try to persuade ourselves that somehow God will find us acceptable? We have irrevocably damaged his good creation. What right have we to think that there is any way we can undo the damage? The past is fixed and unchangeable. Worse, our past actions have in some ways affected the present and also may affect the future adversely.

Why does purity matter? Because God is pure, in a sense which we can only describe in picture language. The apostle John in the New Testament describes God as light without any darkness at all, and makes a similar statement about Jesus. We are given further pictures of Jesus as having a face which shines like the midday sun, and as being the true light which enlightens people. In the Old Testament, coming near to God without being asked was to risk your life.

And yet God is the source of all that is good. Without him there is nothing we can benefit from, no enjoyment, no peace of mind. We need him in a way he does not need us. To come near him, to begin to see things his way, to experience some of his many good gifts, this is our first need if we are to be joyful and peaceful. Without him there is no future and no objective meaning to life, only the mess we get ourselves into as a result of ignoring the creator.

The non-existent spectrum from profanity to purity

We view many qualities on a sort of spectrum. Colors change from violet to red as we move through the visible spectrum. We think of people as varying from tall to short, from thin to fat, from intelligence to imbecility. But we also deal with separate categories, such as male and female, although there are occasionally difficult cases of gender identity.

It is a problem when we deal with categories as though they are on a spectrum, and yet we may do this with good and evil. If something is pure, it is unadulterated with anything else. Contamination, however small, renders it impure. Impurity in one sense is like disease. It comes in many forms and different levels of severity, but it means that you are unhealthy. And however good you try to be, you can never rid yourself of the contamination. You are like a carrier of a disease for life.

When we consider God's purity, one parallel is to think of something which is so much better than our best that we are on a different planet, or in a different galaxy or universe. We are an infinite distance away from his level. The word used to describe this aspect of God is holiness. It means that he is separate from us and uncontaminated by us.

And yet we see differences between human beings. This is correct. Some do worse deeds than others. But we are all on the same planet. The moral differences between us are no more than a few inches, to use the example of distance again; but all of us are light-years from God.

When we begin to look at ourselves in this way, we may understand why God does not ask us to be good or pure in the first place. It is to ask us the impossible. We live on the planet Sin breathing an atmosphere of profanity. If God is to give us an answer to our problems, he must take this into account. Somehow the moral distance needs to be overcome. We cannot reach God, but he certainly has the power to reach us. It is difficult for us to admit that we need help, but it seems only logical if we lack the power to help ourselves.

God came to help us

If we begin with naïve experience, how do we reach purity and moral matters? Morals are a matter of behavior, and we saw that naïve experience poses very basic questions. Before we act in any way whatever, we are faced with making implicit decisions about the nature of reality.

Why is there anything, why is it ordered, complex and sequential, and why are we persons? Our actions depend on our implied answers to these deep questions. If we answer the questions by saying the universe is meaningless, then our actions do not have to be meaningful. On the other hand, any meaning we see in the universe is of great significance if our actions have to relate to it.

As we saw in chapter 5, the limits we experience are also a challenge to us. They also raise the question of meaning and law. If there is no link between reality and morality, then all we can have is the arbitrary and changeable law manufactured by fallible human beings for muddling along somehow. Only if reality and morality are linked at the most basic level can there be any real "ought" in this universe.

The link between morals and reality is exceptionally clear in Christianity. The creation exists because of the action of the Holy Trinity. God *owns* the creation and it is therefore immediately *responsible* to him. Without a God who is a person, there is no basis for our responsibility. If there were any other origin for the universe, it would be impossible to speak of our responsibility in any final sense.

As God made it, the creation is not amoral, nor an undesirable problem because it is material—both of these religious views exist in our world—but positively good and pure because a good and pure God made it. The first chapter of the Bible lays the basis for all human behavior, whether scientific or artistic. But then there was a disaster, which we shall consider in chapter 20. The first human beings disobeyed God. They introduced the profane into human life. Jesus came to put this right. We couldn't do that. What sort of person is he?

The great Christian teacher, C.S. Lewis, said that we do not have many options with regard to our view of Jesus.[5] This is because Jesus claimed to be God. If Jesus was not the God he claimed to be, then either he was self-deceived and as mad as the man who says he is a poached egg, or he was a deceiver of men and as bad as the devil. He was not simply a good man. He never intended to give us that option. The choice for Jesus' identity is between the living God, a madman or a devil. Only if you believe that the early Christians falsified Christianity can you escape this choice. But then, would they have falsified something they willingly died for? Would the apostle Paul—who fully supported the death of Stephen, the first Christian martyr—have become a foremost promoter of Christianity, unless something amazing had happened to convince him of its truth in the form in which we have it?

Again we can see that the super-personality of God is involved. Only God could bring back the missing purity and he was born into his universe as a human being who, not surprisingly, was perfect—the God-man, Jesus—to represent us. We are also told that all things were created through Jesus. As God, he existed *before* the creation and indeed before his human birth.

It is only in the fact of creation by the super-personal God that we find answers to our questions about morals. The frequent moral impulses I have (conscience) are because I was made to be responsible to my maker. This universe is unbounded but finite. The answer to moral questions comes from outside, and that is why men so frequently experience frustration when they try to find the answer inside the universe, as we saw above with environmental questions. The only link with outside is that which a kind creator may have given us. We need to look for his special revelation. What does it say?

---

5. Lewis, *Mere Christianity*, 54-56.

17

Listen . . . is there anyone there?

Reason and experience tell us to listen out for something like Christianity

THERE COMES A POINT in thinking when action is appropriate. The train of thought and observation which leads a geologist to the conclusion that there might be oil underneath him is fruitless in the absence of a decision to drill for it. When a doctor makes a diagnosis, it requires some application to the question of treatment. If there is no action, the thinking is rendered useless.

One of the inevitable questions facing everyone is "Why?" Why is there anything at all? That there is *something*, is an irrefutable naïve experience. As we have seen, there are other such experiences: order, unity and diversity, sequence, personality. The belief that no answer can be given to the question "Why?" is totally without evidence. Indeed, what evidence there is runs wholly in the opposite direction: we live in a universe of logical causes and effects. Why should the parts be accounted for, but the whole remain inexplicable?

The end of reasoning?

If we must come to the end of reasoning at the very point when it is of the greatest significance to us, life is a sad affair to which we can see an ending, but no meaning. If there is no meaning to life, then behavior is likewise without meaning and law has no innate power but is a mere convenience which may be changed or disobeyed at whim. We have seen some of the catastrophic implications of these beliefs in previous chapters.

When faced with the question *why*, what should be the attitude of the reasoning person? If we cannot reason where we or the universe came from, are there any other possibilities? Perhaps we can learn a lesson from the very existence of our naïve experiences. In order to appreciate them, we have first to pay attention to them. Reason is not the first step, but is a reaction to naïve experience.

Evidence but not proof

Translated to the question of our origin, it is certain that we cannot reason from where we are to what may or may not have produced us, although we are able to see that there is some continuity of life which existed before us. But the whole of everything around us, the amazingly complex universe, surely cannot be explained by anything within it? This is like saying that a baby contains evidence of its parents.

And yet a baby *does* contain evidence of its parents written in every strand of DNA in every living cell in its body. Although the parents' existence cannot be proved by this string of genetic coding, yet it is evidence of their action in making the baby. Does the universe contain some evidence of where it came from? We need to pay attention to this universe's implicit messages. What are they?

The first message is that if proof is regarded as absolute total certainty, nothing at all can be proved beyond doubt. That is, human beings will always find a way of disbelieving something if it suits them to do so. We can see this when people convicted of crimes on the soundest of evidence refuse to believe it. Granted, there have been some cases where convictions have been shown to be unsound at a later date. But there are other cases, as at the recent public enquiry into the sad murder of a little girl, Victoria Climbie, in England. One killer accepted guilt and apologized for his crime[1] whilst the other maintained that she was the victim of a plot and refused to acknowledge the overwhelming evidence.[2]

---

1. BBC News, "Climbie killer says sorry."
2. ———, "Killer disrupts enquiry."

The role of a framework

We do not have to look far in this world for evidence that people view things in frameworks, and that the frameworks may be in violent disagreement. Saddam Hussein and Osama bin Laden had very different views from Tony Blair and George Bush. What was viewed by the former as praiseworthy might be considered scandalously criminal by the latter. And frameworks are important when it comes to proving things. In the view of bin Laden, the US and its allies were apparently to blame for the terrorist outrages inflicted on them.

This tendency to blame the victim is not limited to high profile sadists. In rape trials the accused may often claim that the apparent victim encouraged the act, even when she said, "No." So what framework does naïve experience give us? And how may we seek to interpret it, or follow it? This question is at the centre of this book. Can we really detect God's fingerprints?

As we have seen, there may be evidence, but "proof" is obviously a loaded word. Can the evidence also indicate how it should be viewed? The point of naïve experience is that we try to start *before* our mind can somehow put the evidence in a developed framework. This might make it conform to some prior theory which may or may not be correct. We are in the realm of axioms, assumptions or presuppositions.

The essence of a presupposition

It would be easy for me to pretend that starting with naïve experience is a way to avoid the possible distorting effect of presuppositions. But that would not be honest, and I have no wish to abandon the reader's trust. The very words "naïve experience" are loaded with connotation, and I have put much content into them by the arguments in this book.

I am arguing that naïve experience precedes the use of reason, in just the same way as a baby experiences things and later may reason about them, and maybe I am right, but I have no way of proving it. That is why I am asking you to see whether you agree with me. What I can say is open to testing, and you are free to carry out any test you wish. There will always be presuppositions, and they will always be open to test by experiment.

In a way, what I am asking you to do is related to the very concept of naïve experience. It comes to us as a message, and when our powers of reason are exhausted, there is always the possibility of further messages.

If we cannot find an answer to the question, "Why is there anything?" from our naïve experience, then maybe there are further possible experiences which may answer the question. In short, naïve experience may be viewed as something revealed to us, and perhaps we should be looking for further revelations when our cleverness runs out. Incidentally, a revelation does not necessarily mean that a *person* did the revealing. In nature, snow may melt, revealing plants previously hidden. Or a fire may destroy something which previously hid something else. I am simply making the point that we may understand such experiences as revelations *to us*. Scientists are familiar with observations which suggest some new theory, and experiments which are then devised to confirm or refute it.

Revelation consistent with our naïve experience

Consistency is important. If we encounter a revelation which somehow disagrees with our naïve experience, there are two possibilities. Either we are wrong about how we view naïve experience, or the revelation is really a misconception. So if our naïve experience involves something which is ordered, embodies unity and diversity, sequence, and personality, then for the revelation to deny any of these characteristics is a serious point of conflict.

In chapter 6, I argued that we live in a framework of philosophy and history, or to give it human characteristics, reason and experience. We need to find a purported revelation which is philosophically and historically consistent. This gives us potential ways of disproving the purported revelation, and therefore helps us to confirm our knowledge if it is true.

Truth in philosophy and history

I have argued in chapter 15 that Christianity is the only religion of revelation which agrees with the whole of our naïve experience. If we disagree at this point, then you may turn to examine all the other religions, but are likely to find them less satisfactory as I have suggested. But there is still an important matter to be considered. Agreement with naïve experience is an argument in the realm of philosophy. It is a matter of analysis which does not depend on history. It could even be true *without* Christianity being *historically* true. But if Christianity is not historically true, it is false and useless altogether.

What do I mean by "historically true"? I mean that if we are to consider the Bible to be the revelation of the Triune God, then God does not speak lies. The whole of the Christian faith rests on certain purported historical truths. Without them, Christianity is worthless, and its teachings are an illusion, a fantasy. What are these essential truths?

The first historical truth

The question of origins is not a matter of history, as we saw in respect of the evolution argument in chapters 1 and 10. Origins come outside or at the edge of history. But there is the important matter of God's actions within history. After the good creation, we are taken sharply into the fall of humankind. If there was no *historical* fall of human beings, then we have no explanation for the mess which has since occurred in a world which was created good. Estrangement of human beings from God is the Biblical explanation for much of our troubles.

It is not the sole explanation, since we have hints in the Bible that there are created beings of a spiritual nature and that some of these also have fallen and interfere with the originally good creation. Fallenness is something which can only directly affect beings with personalities, but they may have an effect on other created entities. It may be the case that some tendencies we encounter in the natural and physical world are the result of actions by fallen spiritual beings who need not necessarily live within our universe. We need not reject a strict idea of physical causality on this account. The whole universe may have suffered in some ways[3].

The second historical truth

Because of the far-reaching consequences of the fall for all human beings and the world they inhabit, the second historical truth which is necessary for Christianity to be true is the sacrificial death of Jesus Christ. When He died in space-time on a Roman cross outside Jerusalem around AD 33 by our reckoning, Jesus was achieving a cosmic reconciliation with God for all human beings who wanted to be reconciled.

---

3. Rom 8:19–22.

The act is recounted in the Bible under two specific headings. First, Jesus died in the historical framework of Jewish sacrifices as laid out in the Old Testament. Secondly, his death was not simply physical torture, horrific though crucifixion was; it was worse than this because somehow—in a way which we cannot imagine—the person of the Son of God was cut off from the fellowship of love which He enjoyed with the Father and the Holy Spirit. This catastrophic event is viewed in the Bible as the punishment due to all people who reject God from their lives. But the punishment is self-inflicted. As we saw in chapter 15, to reject God is to accept hell. God is the origin of all that is good, and if we reject him, what is left is the absence of goodness and love, namely hell.

When President Nixon referred to the American moon landing in 1969, he called it the greatest event since the creation. Christians would not agree. The greatest event was when Jesus Christ died for human beings. This brings us to the next event which must be historically true if Christianity is to be true.

The third historical truth

When Jesus died on the cross, his followers thought it was the end. They had lost a great teacher, and if God allowed him to die, then maybe he was not what they had been thinking. Perhaps he was not the promised Messiah or Christ despite all the miracles which had apparently authenticated him. How could he have failed to avoid death?

What happened next is the sole reason for the existence of the Christian Church today. The dead Jesus got up, walked, talked, and showed his amazed followers that death could not hold him. As St Paul wrote in his first letter to the Christians at the Greek town of Corinth, "If Christ is not risen, your faith is in vain." Christianity stands or falls on this one historical event.

Some quite ridiculous suggestions have been made by people wanting to disbelieve this historical truth. Perhaps Jesus was not dead? The Roman soldiers who performed the crucifixion knew a dead body when they saw one. In any case, how could Jesus survive when a soldier put a spear into his heart after his apparent death? And what happened to the Jewish Temple guards who mounted watch over the tomb? The Jewish authorities had a vested interest in preventing the body from being stolen. When the followers of Jesus started to preach that he had risen from the dead, why could the authorities not produce a body to rebut this?

Many years ago a lawyer called Frank Morison set out to prove that Jesus did not rise from the dead. His book *Who Moved the Stone?* gives the reasons why he came to the opposite conclusion, and debunks some of the arguments of those who simply want to reject the miraculous. Every single argument against the resurrection made in recent times has been fully answered by Christian writers. These arguments simply hold no water. The motive behind them is to avoid any suggestion of the miraculous in history. I have given an account of a space-time miracle which cannot be explained any other way in chapter 11. In that chapter I have mentioned also Simon bar-Kochba, one of several Messianic pretenders who were *not* raised from the dead and consequently have no followers today.

By far the strongest positive evidence for the resurrection of Jesus is the existence of the church he founded. The Christian faith centers on truth, God's truth, and many early Christians died in nasty ways because they worshipped as God the Jesus who died and rose again. They would under no circumstances "recant". To die for a lie is a ridiculous end to a ridiculous life. Persecution affected the church from the beginning of its existence. The only rational conclusion is that Jesus had been seen alive by many people after his death, as the New Testament describes, and they knew conclusively that he had greater power than had ever been previously displayed in human history. Power so awesome is enough to silence any counter-argument!

So is there anyone there?

If we are to recognize the Bible as God's revelation in words of all that matters for human life, it needs to be consistent with reality and with itself. We can accept that minor copyist errors may have crept into the text, but the evidence for the preservation of the text is impressive. The Masoretes, devout Jews who copied out the Old Testament up to the Middle Ages, were particularly scrupulous over the preservation of what they considered God's words. Archaeological discoveries have shown the Bible to have an impressive textual pedigree. What we have today is substantially the Old Testament which existed in the time of Jesus. Jesus' view on it is given in the New Testament, and his attitude was of total reverence for it as truth.

God's Fingerprints

Why do Christians accept the New Testament as God's revelation? Again, the authority comes from Jesus. He promised his followers that they would be able to remember the truth, and this was to be a specific work of the Holy Spirit. Textually, we have far better archaeological evidence supporting the accuracy of transmission of the New Testament than for any other ancient historical documents.[4] One further important matter concerning the truth of the New Testament is that it is also internally consistent although written by numerous authors.

Intellectual and emotional concerns

The intellectual problem many people seem to have with Christianity concerns miracles. It is hard to see why, when we consider naïve experience. The existence of anything at all is totally inexplicable in itself, and it is only when we reason further (as in this book) that we can perhaps find even one plausible explanation of why there is something rather than nothing.

When we consider the miracle of creation itself and the other miracles within that creation such as the existence of persons and complex ecosystems, there can be little to object to when the performer of those miracles introduces the occasional space-time discontinuity into the universe. After all, it is totally dependent on Him for its continued existence. Obviously we need to be convinced that something is such a miraculous discontinuity, but resurrection of a human body can only be explained in terms such as these.

There are also emotional difficulties for some who find it hard to accept that humanity is wayward and in need of reconciliation with God. But we have a universe in which there is considerable human evil, and unless we are going to adopt a view of evil which says in effect that it doesn't matter, responsibility for evil deeds must be placed with the people who commit them. Others have a problem with the very existence of evil. They ask why it should affect particular persons more than others. Jesus himself repudiated the idea that those who suffer more are being punished for greater wrongdoing. On this perplexing matter, I would like to mention the opinion of an Anglican clergyman who had a young family and who died of cancer a few years ago at about the age of forty. One of my daughters worked as a helper in his parish in Hirwaun in Wales and knew him well.

This minister was interviewed on a BBC radio program, and the interview later won a journalistic award. Russell Chiswell knew he was going

---

4. Bruce, *New Testament Documents*, 9-15.

to die, and the interviewer probed his feelings as a Christian on this matter. He acknowledged that some people would ask the question, "Why me?" in his situation, and gave an answer which showed remarkable insight. "The essence of evil," he said, "is that it is *random*." The unfairness of evil, why one person here suffers whilst another is free from harm, this is all a part of why evil *is* evil.

Christians are by no means free from suffering. They are different from other people because they have a God who cares for them and has experienced earthly suffering, a support system on earth in the form of the church, a basic but clear understanding of the nature of reality, and a perfect future after death but with some of the joy here and now.

The importance of listening

There are many ways of not listening. We can talk ourselves, we can cause another experience to interfere with our conversation, we can think of something else, we can day-dream. We do not have to listen to anything, and nothing, absolutely *nothing*, has any right to interfere with *us* against our will! In the words of a pop group called "The Animals" back in the swinging sixties, "It's my life and I'll do what I want."

There is only one problem. If we do not listen, we may miss something. If someone claims the lottery prize too late, they may lose it. Personally, I don't like lotteries for several reasons. For instance, it seems rather daft to pay hard-earned money so as to be regularly disappointed, and all gambling is clearly aimed at exploiting greed. But I rather like the Jewish joke about a devout Jew who regularly and most sincerely prayed that he would win the lottery. It got to the point where he was tearing his hair out in the synagogue every week. Eventually, a voice from above replied to his anguished outpourings: "I can hear you. But do me a favor. Meet me halfway. Buy a ticket!"

Listening is very important, and if we do not listen, we run the risk of missing something very good. If it comes to having the fullest life possible, there is only one way to proceed. Since the universe does not answer our questions about life's meaning, it makes sense to look out for something or someone who does. Those very questions, if they are not part of the hypothetical "accident" that some people believe in, are perhaps the reason why we should look out for better answers than we can find on our own.

18

The step which matters

A summary of the argument,
and the nature of Christian conversion

LET US SEE WHETHER we can summarize the argument so far. First, there is something rather than nothing. Otherwise we would not have an experience of any sort, and certainly not something which can be discussed as at present!

Secondly, there is an ordered something, not a chaos without order. The order we experience involves unity and diversity, sequence (the experience of time and causality), and a distinction between self and non-self (our identities). This also means that we recognize the self as a person, having certain characteristics which are different from those of a lump of dead rock, and an identity different from all other animate objects.

Thirdly, the use of human minds to theorize is important. If we cannot trust logic, we are doomed to an impossible existence.

Fourthly, logic on its own is sterile and can mislead if we have the wrong starting point. Therefore, experiment is also required: a test of whether the logic connects with our real experience of a real universe.

Fifthly, the universe we live in is ultimately inexplicable in itself. If it is all that exists, it is totally incomprehensible that such complexity and causality can be a "mere accident." We might reasonably ask, "What caused the accident?" Furthermore, in the absence of other externally-determined destinies, the universe has its own apparent end written in to it in one of several feasible ways. If the end of the universe is writ so large into its material, the question of its origin clamors for an answer!

Sixthly, if the universe's origin is to be explained by an external cause, that cause must encompass all that we experience in the universe: existence, order, sequence, unity and diversity, personality. This does not rule out what might be unimaginable and inconceivable (to human beings) also being a part of the cause.

Seventhly, we must accept as true that we cannot prove the existence of God. If he is there, he is greater than the universe, and we cannot argue the existence of the greater in terms of the lesser. We are therefore forced to search within the universe for evidence of his presence. The argument so far has been two-fold: first, that the universe itself points to a greater and separate cause which necessarily encompasses personality (which would otherwise not exist, and neither would this discussion); secondly, that a person who is greater than the universe, and who also created it, clearly has the option of self-revelation within it in any way he chooses.

Eighthly, if we look through human history, the argument of personal revelation is essentially limited to the claims of three religions: Judaism, Christianity and Islam and their offshoots—in the case of Christianity, we are talking about all three major branches—Roman Catholicism, Eastern Orthodoxy and Reformed Protestantism—as mainline.

Ninthly, in essence, what rules out Judaism, Islam and many recent religions derived from Christianity, such as Jehovah's Witnesses and Mormonism, is the nature of the God who is claimed to be revealed within them. In Christianity alone it is claimed that the God who has revealed himself is a person of such complexity that we can only understand him as triune, encompassing both unity and diversity, and therefore encompassing this aspect of the universe. This aspect of the God of Christianity also explains the characteristic feature of love in this religion: the three persons are self-sufficient in love between each other from all eternity, hence creation of the universe was a voluntary act of love, and as one New Testament writer states it, "God is love."[1]

What is a conversion?

So where does this take us? Does it take us anywhere? What is the use of a religion? Is it a device to get what you want, or to make sure there's pie in the sky when you die? These are good questions. To be honest, I have never thought in terms of Christianity as a means of getting anything. I

1. 1 John 4:8.

became a Christian at the age of 16 from a background of agnosticism, which explains why I am sometimes a little hard on people who claim to be atheists or agnostics. Crucial to my conversion was the Christian view of the universe and humankind. Truth was what mattered most to me. I find atheist and agnostic systems impossible to accept because they simply don't seem to fit the world I'm in. But before you turn your theories loose on me as a convert and say that people are converted from one religion to another for various psychological reasons, let me agree with you that psychology is certainly part of it.

Psychology deals with matters of human behavior, and belief systems are one of the things psychologists study. They are often able to tell you a lot about how people change their mind, and what things human beings can do to change other people's minds. This is a fascinating area of study, and in my work, I have touched on it. In particular, I have researched some aspects of how dentists may help people to learn better ways of cleaning their teeth.

How do you change someone's mind? How do you change your own mind?

What stands out very clearly is that giving someone knowledge about how and why they should clean their teeth does not change their attitude, and changing their attitude does not change their behavior. If you want to help someone to do this, the keynote is relevance to *that* person. Indeed, studies suggest that people have behavior packages, and the package into which tooth cleaning comes is called the health beliefs model. It may sound bizarre, but a study many years ago showed that in some teenagers, those who frequently cleaned their teeth also frequently changed their underwear, and *vice-versa*!

One important psychological finding is that it is virtually impossible to change the mind of someone who doesn't want to alter. People are *never* converted against their will. In my case that was certainly true. I didn't become a Christian because someone tried to force me to change. What happened was I recognized the bankruptcy of my agnostic beliefs in helping me to deal with the world I actually lived in. It didn't make sense to say that everything was an accident. It certainly looked better organized than the average accident!

So I was on the lookout for something which would help me. I wanted to be right, or at least, more right than I was, which seemed pretty wrong as judged by the test of the real world. At that early stage, my understanding was fairly simple. (Indeed, some people may think I still am a bit simple!) I thought that the important question was one of identity. Who you are, where you come from and what you mean against the background of the universe, these were basic questions. Next came truth, or rather how you could know truth. There was so much contradiction in what people thought was true, so could this perhaps be linked to the matter of identity—who they thought they were? Thirdly, how should you behave? This, it seemed to me, depended on what you are and what is true.

This was my simple approach to the question of what I should believe and how I should act. I had already learned something about Christianity and also about other religions, because I was curious about them. I had also learned enough of science to know that there was little or nothing in it which contradicted the main points of Christian belief. For instance, Charles Darwin believed in a personal God, at least in the earlier part of his life, though he asked whether he could really trust his brain because it came from monkeys! And many experimental scientists today are Bible-believing Christians and fully accept all the central facts of cosmological and biological evolution.[2]

In real conversion, the first thing which matters is truth

As we saw in chapter 16, there are certain basic ways in which Christianity could, for the sake of argument, be proved false. The Christian faith stands or falls with the historical truth about Jesus Christ. On the negative front, no one so far has made any counter-argument which stands up to examination. On the positive front, it would be quite remarkable if a religion which stands above all for truth had *started* with lies, deception, conspiracy and *the acceptance of martyrdom by its pioneers.*

In contrast with Christianity, some modern religions have quite a problem with truth. There has been considerable revision of the Mormon scriptures,[3] for instance, when copies of the original publications are compared with those now available. This is despite the original claim of Joseph Smith, the founder, to have received a totally accurate version of the Book of Mormon from God. Other Mormon scriptures, such as the purported direct revelations from God in the Doctrines and Covenants, have also

2. Alexander, *Rebuilding the Matrix*, 58-62.
3. Groat, Joel, B. " Changes to Latter-day Scripture."

been changed. Why the revisions, if the original was correct? Is it because of the many embarrassing mistakes? Fortunately, some copies of the earlier versions are preserved!

Then there is the founder of Jehovah's Witnesses, Charles Taze Russell. In a court case in 1913 when he sued for libel and lost, he claimed to know the Greek alphabet. When challenged by the opposing counsel simply to read out letters in this language, he was forced to admit his perjury. In the same case, he perjured himself several times. He was also involved in a money-making scam when the Watchtower Society, of which he owned 99%, promoted expensive "miracle wheat" which was anything but miraculous.[4]

One of the most remarkable things about Christianity is the number of people who have gone into its ministry and have then denied important aspects of Christian truth. We have seen bishops, no less, deny things like the virgin birth, deity and resurrection of Jesus Christ. One wonders why these people have entered an organization with which they disagree so much. Again, their arguments have been thoroughly answered. If they are not convinced, the problem is theirs, not ours. As I have tried to emphasize, no one is forced to be a Christian.

Probability and natural law

When I became a Christian, what struck me was the total impossibility of the "accident" theory of the universe. What, first, is the probability of something coming out of *absolutely* nothing? It has to be zero, the lowest probability. Then what is the probability of something actually existing? It has to be one, the highest probability, because something *does* exist. Then what is the probability of the actual universe we know existing? Again it is one. But what is the probability of development of the present universe from a cosmic singularity, *without* any physical laws? Here we have to consider the complexity of the universe.

Scientists have pointed out the importance of physical constants in our universe. If these constants varied even a tiny amount from what they are, the present complex universe would be impossible. Everything works according to natural law, and the constants are like unbreakable laws and limits. As I have asked before, is everything written into the quarks, leptons and force-carrying bosons? How do these minute entities *know* they have

---

4. Martin, *Kingdom of the Cults*, 34–46.

to obey the laws and physical constants? And how does such obedience lead to the complex universe we enjoy?

As I walked down the road one spring morning towards the station to catch my train to work, the birds were singing, the trees were blossoming and people were walking or driving. The birds were seeking or cementing relationships for future reproduction, according to what David Attenborough and others tell us; the trees were sending out signals to birds or insects that they were ready to indulge in reproduction by the agency of these animals; the people were an amazing group of communicating, technologically aware persons, each one of whom was more complex than we can understand, let alone build. Is it all written in the quarks, leptons and force-carrying bosons? Pull my other leg, it's got bells on!

Conversion, natural law and moral law

My conversion to Christianity was not forced; yet in one sense there was little else I could have done. Only by accepting the "accident" theory could I have an alternative viewpoint, and that is not a satisfying theory. It has implications far beyond the question of what truth is; if the entire universe is an accident, that also affects my *behavior*, as we have outlined already. We shall discuss truth and morals in chapters 20 and 21, but a few further observations may help our train of thought now.

The natural law of the natural world, of which we are a part, is both wonderful and awe-inspiring. There is beauty in stars and galaxies, in the solar system, in the plant and animal kingdoms around us, in human beings, and in human activities from technology to the arts. All of this, in theory at least, can be accounted for in terms of natural law. The rules of mathematics, physics, chemistry and biology are our starting point for understanding this amazing and beautiful complexity.

But there is another form of law around us. It is what we call moral law, and the arguments surrounding it are copious and intricate. It is where we move from the "is" to the "should." People are for ever saying we ought to do this or ought not to do that; a friend of mine who is a psychotherapist has coined the phrase "the hardening of the oughteries" to describe this aspect of human behavior! How can the "is" and the "should" sides of life be brought together?

In scientific terms, there is no way: we are doomed to a total dichotomy of law in our thought (natural law) and action (moral law) if we accept the "accident" theory. If this is true, there can be no basis for moral law other than human preference. As we have seen, there is no clear argument for preserving the human species, or for keeping this world in any particular state of biodiversity, if it is all physically doomed in any case.

It is at this point that the relevance of the Christian explanation becomes even more pressing. Acceptance of the super-personal Creator does not only give us an explanation for the universe, important though that is. It also gives us a moral standard which is self-existent, and which in the Holy Trinity encompasses the superb and all-surpassing quality of love. Not only is God all-powerful, he is also love. Here is the origin of the intended moral standard for human behavior. Without love, St Paul wrote, I am nothing.[5]

Conversion and commitment

What takes place in conversion? It is certainly a turning point: that is what the word conversion means. But what changes? Is it any different from changing your opinion? I used to buy that brand of socks and then I changed to this one. I used to think this channel was good, but now it's deteriorated badly. I used to believe the universe was an accident, and now I believe it was created by the Holy Trinity. Yes, opinion is involved, but there is more, a lot more! My opinions have changed on a very wide range of matters, so much so that I now have a new *method* of forming opinions. Why is that? It is because I now have a new commitment, a new loyalty. The God who made me has recruited me as a willing servant. I can't say I am an obedient servant in every respect, far from it; but yes, I am willing to obey him, which is more than I was when I pretended that God didn't exist.

How was I converted to Christianity? The first stage involved getting to know about it. The main surprise was that it was about Jesus Christ in the first place, not about good behavior, or wisdom or knowledge. It is about how I as a person relate to the person of Christ, the person who is unique by being both God and man. And because I relate to him, I learn how to relate to God the Holy Trinity, and to the rest of the creation including other persons.

The second stage in my own conversion was when I learned in a very simple way about my own most important needs, and made a sensible decision about them. I can still remember one sentence spoken by a leader at a weekend away for young people at the church I sometimes attended. He

5. 1 Cor 13:2.

said, "The average working man is willing to throw his life away for £14 a week." That was an average UK working wage in 1960.

I can remember thinking about the futility of selling your life for *any* sum of money, no matter how great. One life, my life, any life was too remarkable and precious to be viewed in such terms. If there was nothing else, then what was the point of life? Does winning the lottery make people satisfied? It may give them some excitement and even some happiness, but does forty-six million pounds (a recent prize) *satisfy* them? At that point, I realized that no sum of money could satisfy me, because that was not where satisfaction came from. Satisfaction came from having a value in yourself, being in the right place, knowing truth from falsehood, and doing, or trying to do, the right things.

Moving on

Many different people have many different routes as they are converted to Christ. I use his name because it is clear that they transfer their loyalty to him, and not to a mere belief system. It has become common to say that people *convert* to another religion or worldview, but for conversion to Christ it is far more appropriate to say that they *are converted*. I know that I was converted, since looking back I can see that I was not the person who took the initiative.

It was what happened to my thinking and experience that led to my changing paths. Without the signs in the creation, I would not have looked for a better way to live. It was the bankruptcy of my agnostic thinking and the amazing intricacy of the universe which led me to look for a better explanation. If God had not created the world the way it is, I would not have been pointed to a better explanation than "accident." And when I say I looked for a better explanation, I mean that I looked for an explanation that was already there, not one which I invented in some way. There is no doubt that God has spoken directly to some who are his prophets, but for most of us, the other route of simply following the implied questions in our experience is more important.

What happens after a real conversion? I think there are many possibilities, but I have space to list only a few. If my experience was anything to go by, the new convert is deeply interested in all aspects of the new belief-system. For new Christians, the Bible becomes an absorbing literature. The meaning of the Old and New Testaments is of prime importance for daily living.

What do they say, and how does it affect me? Then as now, I read it as God's message to me in human words. I was fascinated by archaeology, and all matters concerning the historical setting of the Bible. As time went on, I started to look at the Bible in its original languages, though this took some time to begin. My linguistic knowledge is still rudimentary, but I have found it gives some help to my understanding.

The church of Jesus Christ

But there is much more to being a Christian than reading the Bible, important and helpful though this is. I was converted out of my pagan environment into the Christian church. I became one of an enormous group of people who all had the same basic belief-system. All of us trusted God, loved him and were beneficiaries of his love. The abiding picture in the Bible is that the church is *married* to Jesus Christ.

This is a remarkable statement. It is a picture of trust, loyalty and love. I was bound in a group of people to my Master, the Lord of all creation. The people are fallible and capable of most types of error and sin. The Master is infallible and a source of constant help for his church. Only by his amazing powers can such a diverse group of people hold together. If you meet people who say it is possible to be a Christian outside the church, they have a very defective understanding of what a Christian is. If they read their Bible, they should see the very important place given to the church. But sometimes the problem is recognizing the church.

Jesus referred to wolves in sheep's clothing when he described those who are apparently in the church but are not part of the flock of sheep.[6] It is impossible to recognize as Christian those who openly deny one of the main Christian truths.

Jesus used the parallel of physical child abusers to describe those who caused young believers to sin or to err, to wander from the truth. He said it would be better for them to be drowned.[7] The writer of the great letter to the Hebrews said that if someone had come close to actually being a Christian and had experienced something of its wonders, but then denied it, they would never become Christian.[8] It gives us pause for thought to realize the serious position of someone who preaches a false gospel.

6. Matt 7:15.
7. Matt 18:1–6.
8. Heb 6:4–6.

The step which matters

    The three historical truths mentioned in chapter 16 are essential to the minimum gospel, as are the philosophical truths of the triune superperson, the origin of the universe, and the entry of Christ into the world in human flesh. Of course, these truths lead on to other truths, but the title of Christian means believing this as a minimum. Thank God that you can be a Christian without being perfect! The basic truth is simple enough for a child to understand it, and Jesus said that we should become Christians like children.

19

Why choose?

The matter of responsibility to God

AT THE HEART OF human existence there is a moral problem. This book has outlined our naïve experience of something that is ordered, complex, sequential and includes persons, and how this leads us towards realizing that there is a super-personal Creator who embodies marvelous qualities like love, and to whom we are *responsible*.

It is the last factor which matters. We may come to the point of conversion, but at this very point we realize that something is wrong. Many do not believe in this super-person, and some are actively hostile to him. One of my daughters spent a year in Albania after she had graduated. She was invited to go with a team of young Christians from her university, in order to give support to Albanian Christians in the universities at Tirana and Elbasan.

Until a short while previously, Albania had operated the most hostile policy towards all religions but unbelief. Christians had had to put up with aggressive persecution from an atheist state. Consequently, when the barriers came down, they were keen to fraternize with young Christians from countries where they had been allowed to flourish.

Flourish? I look at Britain today, and weep for its unbelief. In a land where there has been no significant persecution of Christians for centuries, and where it is even the "established religion," people have increasingly ignored the truth which has been freely available. I marvel in contrast at Christians in those countries where they have been persecuted. Isolated and ridiculed, they have maintained the faith. Why? Because they knew it was true, and furthermore that it led to right behavior. But who defines what is right and what is true? It is God himself, the one whom they seek to obey.

Conversion and repentance

When I was converted to Christianity, there was first of all some housekeeping to do. God's beautiful universe had been damaged because I had ignored him. But ignoring him was a worse problem. How could I say I was sorry, when he had given me clear indications that he was there and that I was responsible to him? Ignoring him was by far the biggest problem. How could I conceivably have called his beautiful handiwork a "cosmic accident," something which was impersonal in its basis, and which had its ultimate origin only in the impersonal? What an insult!

Not only was my relationship with God non-existent, but on that account I was unable to relate fully to other people. We are all hypocrites to some extent at least. We all put up a pretence that when things go wrong, someone else is to blame. It is uncommon for someone to accept guilt for a wrong event. We may even think that after denying God, it is comparatively a lesser fault to wrong a mere created person. But a Christian might say that in doing something gratuitously unpleasant or harmful to another human being, we are insulting the God who made them. And so our acts multiply into a war against God.

This is what Jesus Christ came to put right. His death on the cross was to satisfy the needs of justice, but at the same time to enable us to return, to be reconciled to God. And the first step in such reconciliation is to repent, to ask forgiveness for our errors and the harm we have done, *with the intention of following God's perfect law in the future.*[1] The amazing thing, as St Paul puts it, is that Christ died for us *before* we repented, while we were still enemies of God.[2] Only an intense, passionate and forgiving love could do such a thing. Jesus died for his *enemies*.

The choice before us

So what if we don't repent? God has acted. Why shouldn't we simply carry on without any repentance? Perhaps he needs us more than we need him?

---

1. e.g., Rom 6:1–2; Gal 5:13–25; Eph 2:1–10; Jas 2:14–17; 1 Pet 2:9; 1 John 2:3–6.
2. Rom 5:6–11.

We ignored him before, and Jesus died anyway. To speak this way is to miss the point of the good news, the gospel of Jesus' death and resurrection. Jesus died so that we could be restored to the relationship God intended us to have with him. If we still do not want that relationship, are we puppets which God will nevertheless force into compliance?

The clear answer of the Bible is, "No." If we reject God, as I said before, simultaneously we are accepting hell. God does not *need* us. He who exists as a Holy Trinity to all eternity had no external needs. He created out of *love*. He wanted us to know his love. When we wandered from him, he still loved us and Jesus came to save us, to reconcile us to him. But if we do not want him, the choice of doing without him is our responsibility, and we go to hell because we want to avoid God. God loves us, but he does not *need* us. On the contrary, we need him if we are to have the life he has prepared for us.

Conversion means a new life. In one of his best known discourses, Jesus told a Jewish leader, "You must be born again."[3] The leader, a man named Nicodemus, was taken aback, and indicated it. In fact, Jesus had a lot of his problems with the religious leaders of his time. To be born again has two main aspects: first, there is a new life ahead; secondly, there is no going back. To be born again means the boats have been burned, and retreat is impossible. Your loyalty has changed permanently. Once you have experienced the total *rightness*, the joys of the new life, you are not going to miss the shambles you escaped from!

Suffering may be part of Christian life

Of course things can still go wrong. You can be at fault, and you can suffer through no fault of your own. But have you ever wondered why many early Christians willingly went to a cruel death, torn to pieces by wild animals or burned alive in the Roman arenas, rather than deny their Lord and Master, Jesus Christ? In a nutshell, what they had was infinitely better than the transient pleasures of those who persecuted them.[4] They had eternal life, they had a relationship with one who would care for them even as they suffered, and who would control their pains, and since he was the Lord of creation, there was nothing outside his power. And throughout history there have

---

3. John 3: 1–7.
4. Kiefer, "Polycarp."

been those who have become Christians *because* they have seen the attitude of Christians who suffered.

Why do people suffer? One thing is certain, and that is that it is rare for it to be a punishment from God. When Jesus was asked whether some people who had died unpleasant deaths were worse offenders against God, he replied that they were not; but he went on to say that these disasters were a warning to the rest of us to repent, since God alone could give us true security.[5]

For the Christian, that is a security which operates in all circumstances, including the most unpleasant. My heavenly father is the person who made the universe. No way could I be safer than in his hands, with his tremendous love surrounding me. It is *his* universe, and it would stop without his support. Until he decides to end time, it will continue and he will act in it as he chooses.

In a superb book, Bishop Michael Baughen deals with the matter of suffering in a compassionate and helpful way for anyone who wants to know the Christian approach to these matters.[6] He points out the many misconceptions, and the fact the Bible contains a lot more about suffering than about healing. One very sad thing about atheists and agnostics is that they have no hope, and he mentions the reaction of Freud to the death of his daughter and granddaughter: "I am alone."[7]

I myself saw a little of what this meant at the only Humanist funeral I and my wife have attended. The emptiness and sadness was in no way alleviated by the ceremony. Rather, it made it more acute. On our way out, I said to one of the hosts, "I am a Christian. I simply do not have enough faith to be a Humanist." As a visitor to a church once said, "Christians must be the only people who sing and rejoice at their funerals."

The anger of Jesus Christ

It would be wrong to suggest that the love of God precludes any form of anger in him. If we want to understand something about the emotions of God, we should look at Jesus, who was God in human flesh. To talk of the emotions of God is to use human language to describe something which is by no means so changeable or arbitrary. God's love is deep and permanent

---

5. Luke 13:1–5.
6. Baughen, *One Big Question*.
7. Ibid., 96.

beyond our understanding. His anger on the other hand is described as passing very quickly.[8] It should not be viewed as something uncontrollable, because he is in control. In contrast to our anger, God's anger is always to be viewed as part of his justice and totally perfect actions.

It is instructive to look at times when Jesus manifested anger during his time on earth. I mentioned in chapter 18 that he considered those who damaged the faith of new Christian believers to be as bad as child abusers. Another time when Jesus showed anger was when he threw out traders from the Temple where they were impeding the access of non-Jewish people to the one place where they were allowed in that building. Indeed, careful reading of the gospels suggests there were two times when he did this.[9] His words indicate that he acted angrily because in that place people should have been praying, communicating with God; but money-making, and daylight robbery at that, had replaced it. Here Jesus showed anger at human evil.

Jesus was angry also when he castigated the Pharisees.[10] This group of Jews had done a great deal of good in their preservation of the Hebrew scriptures and in many other ways. They took God's law seriously. But they had gone far beyond the law in making up laws of their own, and this impeded the earnest seeker for God with rules which God had not given. Jesus' anger on these occasions showed how seriously he viewed any obstruction placed before those who really wanted to serve God.

Jesus also showed great anger in his response to the death of his friend Lazarus, which was the occasion of one of his greatest miracles.[11] As far as we know, Lazarus had died of natural causes, and Jesus deliberately delayed coming to see him, in order to show the tremendous power of God over his own creation by raising Lazarus to life again. Yet when Jesus stood outside the tomb, he was greatly moved, and the Greek words show that he wept not with sorrow, but with great anger. Why was he angry? The one obvious reason is that he was angry at death and its damage to God's created people. Jesus came to give life, but that did not stop him being angry at death.

---

8. Ps 30:5.
9. e.g., John 2:13–16; Mark 11: 15–17.
10. e.g., Matt 23.
11. John 11:1–44.

Why choose to follow Jesus Christ?

We come back to the question of this chapter. It should be clear that even if we do nothing, we are making a choice. Without any action, the choice is to remain as we are, alienated from God and with our own route through life before us. God is the source of all that is good, so if we reject him, we damn ourselves. At the same time, if we are left without God at the end, it can be seen also as a punishment for ignoring him, since he then ignores us.

However we view it, if we end up in hell, it is our own fault. He has provided clear signposts and indications that he is there and that we are responsible to him. But most of all, he has provided a way of forgiveness through dying on the cross. If we want to be forgiven, all we have to do is to ask. And in asking, we are agreeing to repent and to change our ways.

Even when Jesus came to his own people, there was not a great surge of repentance and support for him. The main problem appears to have been that they thought the promised Christ would be a political figure bringing them political salvation from the problems of the time. In God's plan, however, the Christ was to bring salvation for people of all nations from the evils of ignoring God, or as it is graphically described, the *slavery* of sin, the human rebellion against God. It is called slavery, because you can't escape by yourself. You need Christ to set you free.

Starting with the most basic experiences we have, I have traced the way that we are led to the super-personal God, and the God-man Jesus Christ. We do not have to achieve any mind-bending intellectual goals, or perform any Herculean task. We are led to a point where we can switch loyalty, where we stop ignoring God and instead start taking account of our position before him. One thing remains, and that is to count the cost of what we intend to do. Jesus advised potential followers to do this. In the next two chapters we shall look at the two matters of truth and morals, which affect all of human life. After that, it will be possible to make an informed decision.

20

Truth and falsehood

Truth and consistency in the Bible

The fear of the LORD is the beginning of wisdom, and knowledge of the Holy One is understanding. (Prov 9:10, NIV.)

TRUTH IS ONE OF two major concerns when we consider the Christian religion. We would obviously expect anything coming from the creator of the universe to be absolutely true. Yet when we consider human involvement in truth, there are several different concepts of truth to consider.

First, there is a concept of absolute truth. This is expressed at its simplest in a mathematical system. If we consider finance, for instance, then we expect £2 + £2 to equal £4. If it doesn't, we are probably being cheated. But it is important that we add the same type of items. $2 + £2 does not equal either £4 or $4. With other figures, we may encounter other rules. For instance, to walk 5 miles north and then 8 miles west gives you a different position from walking 8 miles north and then 5 miles west. When we talk of absolute truth, we need to know all the qualifying details to understand what is meant.

Then we may talk of approximate or statistical truth. In fact, human beings deal with this far more than they may realize. To say that Manchester is 200 miles from London is true to the nearest 100 miles, and also to the nearest 50 miles, but not to the nearest 1 mile. The closer we try to define something, the harder it becomes. We deal in probabilities much of the time. Within the definition "blonde" there are many shades of color, but we

Truth and falsehood

use the term to distinguish a particular color of hair from black, brunette, red, white or silver.

Next, we may talk of exhaustive truth. This is not something we usually encounter, because there is always more to be said about most things. We can describe a person scientifically in terms of biology and psychology, but this omits the description of artistic achievements, socio-economic status and so on. Nevertheless, we may know truths which are true, even if not exhaustively so. It would be correct to describe me as a white Caucasian, though I may never know whether within the last fifty generations my ancestors included someone from another ethnic group.

Literal truth

What is literal truth? This means taking something as an exact description or as "the plain sense," but whilst the term often has this one connotation, there are several other meanings in dictionaries, and in practice there is often considerable room for discussion over what is literally true, or indeed, "the plain sense." Those who insist on the literal truth sometimes hedge it about with all manner of restrictions and limitations. One example is those who insist that the first two chapters of the Bible must be taken literally as meaning a physical creation of the universe, including human beings, by God in seven specified days, as we now understand the 24-hour day on our planet, regulated by the revolutions of the earth on its axis.

There are others who would say that "the plain sense" clearly does not mean this type of creation. They would point to facts such as the creation of light before the sun, and that the word "day" is used in a different sense in the Hebrew of Genesis 2:4, indicating that the original writer of the words intended them to be taken in a very different way.

Scientific truth

Scientific truth constitutes those observations and discoveries which have been made by human beings over recorded history, and which are coherent and testable by experiment. Whilst this form of truth tends to undergo refinement which gives more precision, there are occasions when it undergoes upheaval as new discovery overthrows some former widely-held concept. However, over the twentieth century there has been a long period of consolidation during which much scientific knowledge has been confirmed and counterchecked in many ways.

As an example, the scientific theories of the origin of the universe were three in number in the 1950s. These were the "big bang," "continuous creation," and "expansion-contraction." The first was about a super-dense "singularity" which expanded to give the present known universe; the second postulated that the universe always existed and that new matter was created as it expanded; the third contended that there is a continual cycle of big bang, expansion, contraction, big crunch and so on.

Today, the first theory is widely accepted as correct. The second theory was shown to be incorrect on very good scientific grounds, which included identifying some radiation left over from the big bang, thereby supporting the first theory. The third theory is now widely considered unlikely, as the current most accurate measurements of the expansion of the universe suggest a heat-death (see chapter 5) to be more likely than a big crunch. Thus science progresses and is consolidated. Incidentally, it does not matter which of these theories is correct, so far as Christianity is concerned, because the question of ultimate origins remains for any of them. Why is there something rather than nothing?

We may view the skeleton of science as well-established. Because of what is known, there is an enormous task to put flesh on these bones, and frequent dispute in many specialist areas. It is very rare for any long-established idea to be questioned, though, and almost unknown for the questioning to relate to a significant major concept. But in some areas there is rapid development of new ideas, and plenty of scope for discussion, disagreement and experiment.

Metaphorical truth

This is an alternative to literal truth. For instance, to take the Biblical account of creation once more, some have suggested that the seven days were never intended to be days as we now experience them. They then point out that the account is intended to say that God created everything and that it was good, and that there are interesting, possibly poetic, parallels between the first three and the next three days.

Literal and metaphorical truth cover every concept of truth which I can think of. There may be other kinds of truth, but all of them probably have to be either literal or metaphorical. Scientific truth, if it is properly developed, comes under the heading of literal truth, but there may be places where metaphors are more helpful in depicting it to human minds. For instance, it is helpful to realize that a subatomic particle like an electron acts both as a wave and as a particle. How these truths are reconciled depends on the way our minds work.

Quality and type of truth

In this short discussion, the *quality* of truth may be described as absolute, statistical or exhaustive. The *types* of truth may be literal or metaphorical. Literal truth may have any quality, but metaphorical truth probably can never be called exhaustive.

In the Christian framework, God is the origin of all that is true. Jesus referred to himself as the way, the *truth* and the life.[1] We have seen in essence how we come to the Bible as God's revelation to human beings. It is bound up with the authority of Jesus as God the Son.

Because Jesus viewed the Old Testament, the Hebrew Bible, as God's truth, and said such things as "until heaven and earth disappear, not the smallest letter, not the least stroke of a pen, will by any means disappear from the Law until everything is accomplished," his views are quite clear. If we accept Jesus' authority, we accept the Old Testament as truth.

The New Testament is a work which shows how in many respects the prophecies of the Old Testament have been fulfilled in history. It is solidly based on the idea that Jesus is the prophesied Messiah, the Christ. In addition, it contains statements of Jesus about the work of the Holy Spirit, such as, "When he, the Spirit of truth comes, he will guide you into all truth."

In the New Testament, authors sometimes make statements to the effect that what they are saying is the solemn truth. When Jesus had just died, the apostle John, in his gospel, described how a soldier put his spear into Jesus' side on finding that he was dead, and then wrote, "The man who saw it has given testimony, and his testimony is true. He knows that he tells the truth, and he testifies so that you also may believe."[2]

---

1. John 14:6.
2. John 19:35.

What are the checks that the Bible is true?

Obviously, it is of prime importance to know that the Bible is true, if it is God's revelation of his truth to human beings. Sometimes people say, "But this is a circular argument. You Christians say that the Bible is true because Jesus said it was. But then you rely on the Bible to tell you what Jesus said!" This matter is important, and there are at least three things to say in response.

First, there is the question of internal consistency. It would be very surprising in the circumstances if the Bible did not record the words of Jesus, and they need to agree that the Bible is true if we are to pay any further attention.

Secondly, there are other checks on truth. We need external consistency also, and agreement with other facts outside the Bible if it contains truth about the real world we live in. We looked a little at the way some atheists try to discredit the Bible back in the first chapter. Thirdly, as we have seen, it is just such views as contained by the Bible to which we are led by the evidence of our naïve experience.

In short, if it is true, the Bible needs to be internally consistent, it needs to be consistent with any external evidence we have, and it needs to tell us things in agreement with our naïve experience. The claims in the Bible are profound and if true, are very compelling. In a book of this length, the reader can hardly expect me to give anything approaching an exhaustive account of why I am convinced of the truth of the Bible. There are far too many matters which I have considered in over fifty years of being a Christian for me to mention more than a few.

I must say in passing that I am even more convinced of the truth of the Bible than I was when I was first converted. But I will give some examples of why the Bible fulfils the three requirements I have listed above—consistency with naïve experience, internal consistency, and consistency with external evidence. If the Bible exhibits these three types of consistency, it goes a long way towards showing that it is true. And if it is true, it is telling truth about both God and human beings.

The Bible is consistent with naïve experience

Under this heading, I think there is a strong argument for saying that *only* the Bible is consistent with naïve experience. If we consider other documents claiming to tell us that the truth about God is *different*, there comes a point where we may have to say that either they are false, or our experience is a delusion which is leading us astray. If the first is the case, then we rightly abandon them; but if the second is the case, we have an impossible dilemma.

We cannot abandon our naïve experience, for it is a part of our lives; how can it be a delusion? There are religions where it is claimed that the material world is illusion or evil, or an encumbrance on the soul. In the Bible, the material universe is absolutely central to God's dealing with us, and it was created real and good, and furthermore *we* are material and have material needs.

What are the ways in which we may see the Bible's consistency with our naïve experience? The presence of *something* rather than nothing is given an explanation in the form of creation, but with an origin in the creator's action. The nature of that *something* as ordered, with limits, cause and effect, unity with diversity, and containing personal beings such as ourselves, is all given a Biblical explanation in terms of the totally free, unlimited super-personal God of Christianity. We actually experience God's love in each joy life brings. The presence of evil as a consequence of the breaking of God's perfect law, we shall consider in the next chapter. In passing, the creation separates evil from the creator, who is good; without this distinction, there is no basis for preferring right to wrong.

The rationality of the truth that God is a Holy Trinity

We have seen in this book how our naïve experience leads us toward one particular sort of God who is a creator and also upholder of us, and everything around us. It has been a frequent criticism of the Christian faith that God is seen as one and also three persons in that one. People have described it as irrational, and sometimes even mistaken what it represents, as apparently in the Qur'an,[3] which dates from the seventh century. A superbly-argued view concerning the nature of the Holy Trinity was made by the fourth-century Christian father Athanasius, bishop of Alexandria, as explained in Peter Leithart's recent excellent book.[4]

It is in no way irrational that God is a super-personal being, greater than our minds can fully comprehend; the reasons why God is like that are

3. Qur'an, Sura 5:116.
4. Leithart, *Athanasius*.

obvious enough if we consider that he embodies love, and that before (to speak in human terms) there was ever any creation he was complete and perfect in his eternity without having to create anything.

The criticism of irrationality should be returned to those who object in this way to the Christian faith. We should ask those who believe that God is a simple unity (rather than a complex unity) to explain how this can possibly be the case in respect of his self-sufficiency and perfection.

How Christians came to understand about the super-person of God

In fact, the early Christians' understanding of the Holy Trinity came as they began to understand the many truths which had been opened to them by the life, death and resurrection of Jesus. They had no easy task in putting it all together.

In the first place, Jesus claimed to be the Son of God. In the Hebrew mind, this was a claim to be of the same nature as God, rather than a statement of inferiority to God as modern Europeans and Americans might think. Jesus used the personal name of God revealed to Moses, "I am," to refer to himself. It is not surprising that one of the charges made against Jesus by his opponents was of blasphemy. In chapter 15, I have already mentioned the Trinitarian implication at the end of Matthew's Gospel in the words of Jesus to his followers.

Secondly, in the letters of the New Testament writers Jesus was considered equal to the Father; for instance in the letter of Paul to the Christians at Philippi, he refers to Jesus who was equal to God, yet humbly came to die on the cross; in the letter to those at Colossae, Jesus is explicitly described as the image of the invisible God. In short, God the Son has everything which constitutes God. As a further example, he is strikingly referred to in the book of Revelation in words directly drawn from an Old Testament passage in the book of Isaiah,[5] referring in strict terms to the God who *alone* is God: "I am the first and the last."[6] Then it continues: "I am the living one. I was dead, and behold! I am alive for ever and ever."[7]

Regarding Jesus, the early Christians came to the conclusion that he was both God and man; regarding the Holy Spirit, the evidence forced them

---

5. Isa 44:6.
6. Rev 1:8.
7. Rev 1:17–18.

Truth and falsehood

to conclude that he was a third divine person. But God in his perfection, they knew from the Hebrew Bible, is one; hence the conclusion that God was a complex person: three persons in one God. Really, when we think of how great God is to create and interact with this universe, could we expect him to be less than a super-person?

The Bible is clearly consistent with our naïve experience, then, and we need look no further than the person of God in the Bible to find details which confirm that this revelation relates to the real world around us. It is *this particular* God toward whom our naïve experience points us.

The internal consistency of the Bible

This is a huge subject, and there are two issues to be distinguished. First, has the text been accurately transmitted down to the present day? Secondly, is there inconsistency in the actual details of the text? Under the first heading, there are known examples of textual ambiguity in many parts of the Bible. Usually, these are so minor as to make no difference to the meaning of the text.

In the well-known statement of Jesus, "It is easier for a camel to go through the eye of a needle than for a rich man to enter the kingdom of God," does it really matter whether the original Greek word is "camel" or "cable"? Either of these alternative readings points to a very difficult task, and Jesus made his point either with a humorous remark (camels don't go through needle eyes), or with a matter-of-fact remark (a cable is much thicker than a thread). Jesus' meaning has been transmitted, though it is uncertain which word is the original.

There are more difficult problems when we consider translation into other languages. For instance, the Septuagint is a Greek translation of the Hebrew Bible made for Jews in Alexandria, and dating from the middle of the third century BC (the first five books) to some time before 117 BC (the rest). Because we have a very accurately transmitted text of the Hebrew Bible, called the Masoretic text, it appears likely that the Septuagint is very accurate in most places, and inaccurate in some others.

What this means is that today we should take the very best texts we have of the Hebrew Old Testament and the Greek New Testament if we want to be sure of the meaning of a Bible statement. In practice, preachers preparing a sermon in English for an English church service frequently do this. They seek to understand the original meaning before preaching

God's Fingerprints

about a statement from the Bible. Of course, for routine understanding of the Bible, we all make use of the best English translations available. Today, for instance, I use the New International Version, which is very good for conveying the meaning of the original Bible at present, though it certainly has occasional imperfections!

Once we have the best text, there may be other problems. I am going to discuss two of these to illustrate how different accounts may be brought together to corroborate each other, even though they may say apparently different things at first sight. The principles involved are of much wider application.

Chronology—an acid test for accuracy

In the Old Testament, there are numerous dates by which events are given their historical reference-points. In the early study of the histories from the time of King David (around 1000 BC) to the time when the whole nation of Israel was taken into exile in Babylon (by 587 BC), it was noticed that sometimes there appeared to be quite large discrepancies in the dates of certain events. This problem occurred particularly in the account of those times when the nation of Israel was divided into two: the northern Israel, and the southern Judah.

Most dates were recorded by the reigns of the successive kings in the two lands, and each land cross-matched its dates with the other. Certain dates derived from different lists varied by as much as forty-five years. Some commentators looked at the numerous apparent discrepancies and decided the texts were simply full of errors. Incidentally, this was to ignore what was known about the thoroughness with which ancient cultures sought to record events which mattered to them. Scribes were trained in the arts of precision and accuracy, and only the best scribes were employed on the most important tasks.

The matter was given a full and scientific examination by a scholar called Edwin Thiele in the 1950s.[8] First he established an absolute reference date for an ancient battle by using astronomical data and Assyrian records. Then he looked at the Biblical accounts of the two different kingdoms of Israel and Judah, and used good archaeological data about them and the other lands around them. Gradually the truth began to emerge.

---

8. Thiele, *Mysterious Numbers*

Truth and falsehood

First, there were two different systems of dating in a king's reign: year 1 could be the year in which the king came to the throne, or it could be the year afterwards (with the first year as a separate accession year). On its own, this could make some substantial differences after a few reigns. Use of one system or the other depended on what was used by the dominant external nation (such as Egypt or Babylon, for instance).

Secondly, there was sometimes a system of co-regency. The heir to the throne might have a reign which overlapped that of his predecessor. This could give very different reckonings for the same date. Thirdly, the year might begin at one place in the year or six months later with different systems.

With all this archaeological data, Thiele established an excellent system of dating for that period of middle eastern history. He even found some places where the Masoretic scribes (who recorded the Hebrew Bible so well) had been worried by apparent discrepancies in the text and made their own emendations, which Thiele was then able to correct.

The moral is that when faced with apparent inconsistency in the Bible, we should look at the full context of the events in question and see whether facts emerge to reconcile the disagreement. In the next example, a New Testament scholar rightly used this approach to solve quite a different problem.

The five accounts of the resurrection of Jesus

In the Bible, there are five different accounts of details about the most stupendous event in human history. It is not surprising that we should have them because without the resurrection, there would be no Christian church. However, there have been numerous attacks on these accounts because at first sight they differ in a number of matters.

The accounts are found in the four gospels and St Paul's first letter to the Christians at the Greek city of Corinth. All of these were likely to have been written within forty years of the earthly life of Jesus; the most cogent argument that this is so came from a liberal New Testament scholar who noted that the sacking of Jerusalem by the Romans in AD 70, an event predicted by Jesus, was nowhere mentioned as fulfilled in these documents.[9]

Because the written documents were available within the lifetime of many of those who had known the events, it is improbable that they would have been accepted by the early Church without correction if there were

9. Robinson, *Redating the New Testament*.

known errors in the accounts. However, it poses a problem for the historical details of what actually occurred, and in what order. If we proceed in the belief that the details are sound—that is, literal truth but not exhaustive truth—there are difficulties in fitting them together.

A most convincing reconciliation of all the details of whom the risen Jesus appeared to, and when, was published in 1984 by a New Testament scholar, John Wenham, who had spent much time in Jerusalem and was familiar with all the places involved. One hard-nosed reviewer referred to it as a "brilliant book."[10]

Wenham first established some probable facts not directly referred to by the five writers concerned. These included the identities and relationships of people among Jesus' followers, and the locations of places where they lived in and around Jerusalem. Such particulars would have been well known to the early church, though it was important to keep personal details secret because of the severe persecutions which often fell upon Christians.

From these preliminaries and the Biblical writings, Wenham was able to reconstruct a plausible complete narrative of all the post-resurrection events which included everything in all five accounts. The five different writers all give selective accounts, but they can clearly dovetail in the way Wenham shows. Incidentally, this gives additional evidence that the resurrection was not a fabrication, as each of the five accounts is written from a different point of view, *and yet* they all fit together logically.

Personally I think that Wenham's account may be correct, but this is not the point at issue. He was answering people who called the accounts "impossible to reconcile." Obviously he *has* reconciled them, and with due attention to *all* the available evidence. Whether he is fully correct is not something we can judge, but at least the accounts can no longer be called inconsistent. Internal consistency has been established for an important part of New Testament history.

In the two millennia since the New Testament was written, there have been many attacks upon the internal consistency of the Bible. Many of these attacks are the result of ignorance about the culture in which the documents were written, and some result from an inadequate knowledge of the New Testament itself. The two examples I have given must suffice here, but many more are available to readers.

---

10. Wenham, *Easter Enigma*.

External consistency of the Bible

There are at least two aspects to this subject. Because the Bible is made of historical documents arising in various cultures, some aspects of the truth of those documents can be tested against other archaeological finds. There is a huge supporting background of Biblical archaeology attesting to the truth of the documents. We shall look first at one example of how archaeology provides confirmation of the truth.

Secondly, we shall look at the question of scientific and historical consistency of the first three chapters of the Bible. The Bible was never written as a scientific document, but there are those who seemingly wish to view it as such. If only they would read the Bible as it is written, they would never come up with the views they have read into it! To believe in a seven literal days creation, as I have already hinted, is to misunderstand what is actually written in Genesis, the first book of the Bible.

Ages and their meaning

At the end of the book of Genesis, it is recorded that Joseph, the Israelite patriarch who died in Egypt where he had been second in command to the Pharaoh, was one hundred and ten years old. Is this true as we would understand it? Now it is possible that he did live as long as that, and there are recent examples of people living longer. But there is an alternative explanation which also fits.

Joseph died in the Egyptian culture, probably around 1700 BC. In common with other ancient cultures, numbers sometimes took on a special meaning. In the book of Revelation chapter 4, there is reference to the "seven spirits of God" in which the word seven refers to completeness so that the term refers to the Holy Spirit. There was also a special meaning to Joseph's age in the ancient Egyptian culture. In our language it is best translated as "a ripe old age."

Other age problems seem to occur earlier in the same book of Genesis. Some persons are recorded as living several hundred years, which is clearly longer than any people of the present day. It is possible that some earlier people *did* live much longer (though biological considerations suggest not) because this may be looked upon as a direct intervention of God to reduce man's lifespan.

However, it is interesting that ages as great as those in the Biblical book of Genesis are given for various ancient kings in Mesopotamia on the Sumerian King Lists, which come from a very different culture. One such king—Enmebaragisi of Kish—was real enough to leave an inscribed monument, and he is reported to have reigned nine hundred years.[11] Though we do not know the actual meaning of these great ages, the individuals to whom they referred were real historical people.

The greatest age recorded in Genesis is that of Methuselah at 969 years; obviously there are no grounds for considering him fictitious purely on account of his reported age, which might have a significance different to mere longevity. The moral is clear. Recorded ages do not have to mean the same in every time and culture, and the Biblical data are consistent with external archaeological sources in recording individuals who reached a great age.

The meaning of the earliest chapters of the Bible

Our next example of the external consistency of the Bible is important in that it covers matters which are of great significance in relation to ourselves. The opening of the Bible sets the scene for us to understand why we are obligated to God, what went wrong in human history and why we and our world are what they are today.

As we look at the first three chapters of Genesis, which describe the creation and the fall of humankind, let us note first that they were written in a culture of great antiquity and very *different* from our own. Secondly, if they are part of God's written revelation to all people in all subsequent times, they have to be in terms which will be *understandable*. Thirdly, the person or persons who wrote them were not *stupid*, and had a purpose in writing which also fulfilled God's intentions.

The different culture means that we cannot necessarily take present day concepts and read them back into the text of Genesis. For the writings to be understandable and therefore fulfill God's purpose of communication, their message must also be clear and obvious. Because the writers were not stupid, it is not acceptable to presume that they wrote things which are self-contradictory or nonsensical. If there are apparent contradictions, they should be examined to see why they are there.

---

11. Kitchen, *Ancient Orient*, 40.

Some scholars in the past suggested that there are two interwoven accounts in these chapters, where an editor has tried to bring together two revered but contradictory early documents in order to create a new combined (but inconsistent) account. They have suggested this on the basis of two different names used for God, but without a scrap of archaeological evidence in the form of copies of those supposed accounts. This was one of the opinions of Wellhausen, mentioned in chapter 1. That earlier documents may be incorporated in the book of Genesis is perfectly possible, but to suppose they were edited by someone who was stupid is going far beyond the evidence we have—the writing itself. What do we find if we examine it?

The seven day framework

Many have remarked on the literary form of Genesis 1:1—2:3. This is clearly poetic, and is put in a seven day framework. But what do the days mean? In the Hebrew text of the second chapter (though not in the NIV translation), the word "day" is used in two other senses also.

If someone says that the days are absolutely literal throughout, then there is a definite contradiction. The framework refers to six days of creation followed by a day of rest, but in Genesis 2:4 there is a reference in the original Hebrew to "the day"—one single day—in which the heavens and the earth were created. It is notable that this is *correctly* translated in the King James "authorized version" translation of 1611. Is it six literal days or one literal day? Why force this contradiction by saying that all the days are literal?

Again, in Genesis 2:17 in the Hebrew text (and also not in the NIV translation) the word day is used. The ancient King James translation again best conveys the Hebrew here: "in the *day* that you eat of it [the fruit of the tree of knowledge], you shall surely die." In company with the eminent Christian geneticist RJ Berry,[12] I am inclined to say that this is a literal use, and that Adam and Eve died *spiritually* on the day when they disobeyed God. And of course, St Paul refers to the new *spiritual* bodies which Christians will have when they are eventually raised from death.[13] However, those who insist that there was no physical death before the fall of the human race have another dilemma: they must either say that this day is not literal, or accept that it does not refer to physical death.

12. Berry, "Rejection of the Creator," 39–45.
13. 1 Cor 15:42–46.

Another point which Berry makes is that the creation of *spiritual* man may have been a second stage alluded to in Genesis 2:7, with God first making existing natural man and then making him a being with spiritual life. The existence of biologically human remains long before Adam, who can be placed from Biblical and anthropological evidence as a farmer in the New Stone Age, around 10000 BC,[14] is an added pointer to this possibility.

Let us now consider the days in Genesis 1, and in passing remind ourselves again that the writer was not stupid. If we accept that, then the account is not literal. Light was created on the first day. But light comes from the sun and the moon. These were not created until the fourth day. Incidentally, how can you have a literal day without a literal sun? This is a poetic parallelism; the writer was not stupid. There are also parallels between the second and fifth days, and the third and sixth days. All this has been noted in far more detail by previous writers.[15]

The intention of the seven day framework

What is God's intention in giving us this poetic framework? One of the most obvious reasons at the present time is that he intended the framework to be acceptable to all cultures of humanity at all periods of history. The framework is as acceptable to us in an age when physicists and biologists have delved deep into cosmology and prehistory, as it was in the time when it was first written thousands of years ago, and perhaps on clay tablets.

And what lessons is God teaching the readers of this sublime passage? He is not giving a science lesson on the origins of the universe. Those are probably so far beyond our full understanding as to be incomprehensible to the cleverest scientists among us today. How do you even imagine creation of something where there was previously absolutely nothing? Or the creation of time? So what lessons may *any* reader take home from Genesis 1:1—2:3?

The first obvious truth is that although we cannot understand what creation means, God did it. Into a hitherto non-existent space-time, his immense power brought into existence the entire physical universe with its laws and its potential for development of the wonders we know today. The big bang had physics, chemistry and biology written into it and though we find the origin inconceivable to our finite human minds, the development

---

14. Pearce, *Who was Adam?* 22.
15. e.g., Blocher, *In the Beginning*, 39–59.

of the complex universe may be explored today. Evolution is one of God's great marvels; how could the gradual unfolding over several billion years of all that lives today occur without his continual guiding and supporting presence? He wrote the laws; the universe obeys him!

Secondly, God's creation was *good*. It is pointless to misread our human feelings in relation to this sublime description. Was there *physical* death before the fall of the first human beings? Of course there was. Even in terms of a literal six-day creation, the invertebrate-eating birds created on day five will have needed food before day six! Is it good for us to eat? Of course it is. Is it good for carnivorous animals to find food in other animals? Of course it is. Is it likely that animals suffer in the same way as human beings? Of course it is not. Do animals have a personality like ours? Of course they do not. Is it good to be kind to animals? Of course it is; otherwise we degrade ourselves.

What is the origin of any suffering which may occur in animals? If this came before humanity fell, then it is quite possible that spiritual beings are responsible, fallen angels who hate God. God's creation was good, and the text repeats it over and over again. However, there are clear allusions in other parts of the Bible to fallen angels. Though they are not included in the passage we are considering, we should realize that others beside human beings may do evil.

Philosophy, and the start of human history

As Genesis 1:1—2:3 gives us the account of the *origins* of the universe in the will of God who created it, so the remainder of Genesis 2 leads us into the *history* of human *spiritual* beings. Again, there may be poetic forms in this passage, but there are five main subjects. The start of civilization is given a space-time context. Human beings are given a special relationship with the creator. One command is laid on them for obedience. Other tasks are given to them in relation to plants and animals. Woman is given a special place in relation to man, and marriage is introduced.

These passages, giving an account of origins and the initiation of human history, are unique. For instance, in the ancient Babylonian creation epic, the *Enuma Elish*,[16] there are originally at least three gods, and more come later. Two of the originals are primeval seas. There is a pre-existing background from which the earth is made. Man is made as an afterthought

16. Speiser, ANET, 60-72.

to work for the gods as a servile being, and man is not made good, but with evil in him. There is no trace of what we find in Genesis, that human beings are made in the image of God, with a special relationship to him.

As remarked earlier, some have supposed there are two conflicting accounts of creation in these two chapters. In fact, the first so-called "account" is a statement of the origin and quality of the creation, which we may call a *philosophical* description; the second is leading us into the start of recorded human *history*. There can be no other reason for the statements locating man in the Garden of Eden and relating it to the Ancient Near East.

To digress briefly, we have no reason to suppose that man in the biological sense is necessarily identical with man in the image of God (spiritual man). The latter clearly came later, and is not an animal, as were his predecessors.[17] To say that man was created from the dust of the earth is simply to cut out the process by which that was achieved, and which would have been incomprehensible to the earliest readers. A similar foreshortening is seen occasionally in Biblical genealogies, where sometimes several generations are cut out.

The cataclysm at the beginning of history

In chapter 3 of Genesis we are given an account of an event of far-reaching significance for all humanity. The first human beings made in the image of God were tempted to disobey him and did so. As I have said, we are given indications of other beings disobeying him also, and in this passage, one of them is referred to as the serpent. Although the account may be written in a particular form so that all people in all times can understand it, there is no doubt that it is intended to refer to a particular space-time event. This is also taken for granted in other parts of the Bible.

Why were the first human beings given a special command? Why were they tempted? Why did they fall? And why did it have an effect on all subsequent people? These questions go to the heart of the question of trust we mentioned in chapter 4. God wanted us to trust him, but he also wanted to trust us. A command requiring obedience is a good test of trust. It is interesting that the tree is of the knowledge of good *and* evil. The first people knew what was good. They had yet to encounter evil. Sadly, the encounter *involved* them.

---

17. Berry, "Rejection of the Creator," 41–42.

The fall occurred because people given a definite command by their maker disobeyed him. Not only did it affect them, it contaminated all subsequent people. In this world we talk of biological diseases as caused by genetic factors or environmental factors or both. A disease may be programmed into us to emerge at some point in life, or it may be caused by something we encounter, like a germ or tobacco smoke. We may say of sin that once human beings were involved in it, its spread was inevitable. In moral terms, there is often a spread of undesirable behavior to the point where it no longer shocks us.

From truth to morals

Without God and not wanting him, human beings are in a pitiable state. They need good to live, yet so often they choose the bad. It is because of their estrangement from God who is the source of all good that their lives are so ambivalent. The fall is one of the great consistencies of the Bible with external evidence. There is no other satisfactory explanation of why humanity is in a mess.

Thus we are brought to the question of right and wrong. Morality is seen as an answer to many of our problems today, and also paradoxically as the source of some of them! Several times I have alluded to the problems raised when morals are merely left to human preferences. Is there no stronger basis for right human behavior? In the next chapter we shall examine this question.

21

Right and wrong

Why loving God is the true basis for morality

As I POINTED OUT in chapter 4, people want things to be *right*, but they do not agree on what *is* right. Human consensus is not possible. Let us take the crime of murder as an example. It is defined in English law as taking someone's life with premeditated malice. Can everyone agree on this as a crime? Unfortunately, no. We need look no further than Islamic suicide bombers to see that they view their actions as a direct route to paradise, and those who make use of them would commend their actions.

But is suicide bombing perhaps an act of war? Well, that is how the terrorists would see it, but many other people would not. For them, war is aimed at the armed forces of an opponent, not against helpless civilians, though the latter may die without being directly targeted. I can remember an unpleasant British interviewer asking an American after the 2001 attack on the World Trade Center in New York and the Pentagon in Washington whether the US had brought the attack on itself by its actions in other parts of the world. He replied politely, "Excuse me. We do not hijack airplanes full of defenseless people and fly them into large buildings full of other defenseless people. There is a difference between acts of war and acts of terrorism."

What about other crimes? Stealing? It depends how you do it and who you steal from. I previously mentioned Robin Hood as a controversial example. Rape? Well, juries have been known to acquit men accused of this when they have had previous sexual relations with the woman concerned. Abortion? This used to be a serious crime in UK law, with a maximum sentence of 14 years' imprisonment, but today abortion is legally performed in clinics for many reasons, and those who interfere with such clinics are instead breaking the law. And so the list goes on. Take almost any crime and you will find there is no human consensus.

Is education the answer?

But would human consensus be a good thing? Perhaps it might. What is the time-honored method of breeding consensus? It is education. Now I think education is a good thing. I have had a career in education. But does it make people better? Does it help them to see that it might be better if we all refrained from robbing each other, or using violence towards each other?

Well, not really. When it comes to crime, young offenders have often said that they do it for the *excitement*. So when the opportunity arises, they forget that someone else is going to suffer and go ahead with the crime for the thrill. To judge from the last hundred and fifty years of education, all it has done for crime is to produce cleverer and better-educated criminals!

Education is no answer to the problems of crime. This is unfortunate because the British management of criminals is based on a prison system which seeks to re-educate at the same time as they are punished by deprivation of liberty. The Home Office seeks to reform criminals. A few, perhaps, do not re-offend. But what about those who are never caught? And is there any evidence that this policy has any effect on crime? How does it compare with the policy of zero tolerance for crime in New York, where the streets were made safer than they had been for a long time? The basic problem is that people do not change.

Whatever the improvements in technology, the achievements of great scientists, artists, musicians, and writers, however skilful and amazing the successes of sportsmen and sportswomen, however beautiful our possessions and surroundings, *morally* everyone is in the stone age, always has been, and always will be to the end of the world!

Human consensus is a problem

Education has failed to deal with crime. What is wrong is not that there is no human consensus, but that we seem to rely on one. The laws of Britain are made or altered by an elected Parliament which is answerable to the nation at the ballot box. A representative Parliament is unable to create a consensus if the nation does not have one. Man-made laws are man-changeable laws. What was illegal may become legal. Consider the change of laws on homosexuality over the last fifty years, and the current campaign to legalize cannabis. The shifting sands of law are the result of the majority changing its mind. Consensus does not work and may lead to strange decisions.

I once read a story told by a nuclear strategist.[1] In his story, a committee of three people went to the butcher to buy cold meat for sandwiches in bulk for a picnic. The butcher at first said that he had ham and turkey. They conferred and decided on turkey, but the butcher then noticed he also had chicken available. So they conferred again and decided that because chicken was available, they would not have turkey, but ham instead! There is always potential for committee decisions to appear irrational, even though individual members may act logically, and the writer gave the logical reasoning behind the strange decision. Some of our laws may be the result of this phenomenon.

Law, deterrence, reform and morality

There is a further problem with the *application* of law. It is a common view that harsher sentences may deter criminals, although there is little evidence to support this. But in the eighteenth century, many crimes were punishable with death in Britain. What was the result? Many juries simply acquitted the accused because the punishment was out of all proportion to their crimes. There are numerous factors which may affect the application of consensus law.

But can we say that deterrence is morally right?[2] For deterrence to be a useful side-effect of punishment is one thing, but was it morally right to hang someone who stole a sheep in the eighteenth century? It surely is morally wrong to punish criminals *more* than is just for their crimes, in order to have some indeterminable effect on persons unknown who might be contemplating the crime in question. It has been shown that certainty of detection has a greater effect on potential criminal behavior than the harshness of punishment; after all, if you are very unlikely to be caught, why worry about the severity of the sentence? Murder figures varied little in the UK after the death penalty was abolished in 1964.

1. Kahn, *On Thermonuclear War*, 120–122.
2. Lewis, "Humanitarian Theory." 39–44.

It is also immoral to make reform the aim of punishment.[3] It is merciful to release criminals early if they were initially given a fair sentence for their crime and later show remorse and reform. It is quite unmerciful to have an indeterminate sentence which can *only* be ended if remorse and reform are demonstrated. You should not try to force criminals to do something which may be impossible for them. In addition, those who have been wrongly convicted and then protest their innocence are actually penalized further by such a system, as has been shown by a few cases going back to the 1970s.

Justice and consensus

So what is the only moral aim for punishment? It is justice, pure and simple. Justice is served only by matching the penalty to the crime. To increase a sentence for reasons of deterrence or reform is simply unjust. These two effects, if they occur as a result of justice, are welcome, but it is unjust and immoral to make them the reason for a punishment.

Yet this form of immorality occurs today in our system of justice. It results from the consensus, presumed or real. When an unpleasant crime becomes prevalent, like mugging people for mobile phones, the response is to increase sentences to deter people from committing it. Maybe a greater sentence would fit the crime better, but the usual reason given is deterrence. The criminal sentenced according to this principle might correctly say to the judge, "This is not fair. You are victimizing me by giving me an unjust sentence. You want to deter others, but you are making me suffer more than I deserve, in the hope of making other people behave better."

It is not my aim to discuss the complexity of crime and sentencing, but it is clear that some of our problems today result from the ways in which our laws have been constructed. Lawyers say that hard cases make bad law, meaning that the extremes should not be used as the basis for legislation. There will always be legal problems, but let us all aim at justice first.

God's Law

In the seventeenth century, a brilliant man called Samuel Rutherford wrote a classic book on constitutional government—*Lex Rex*—law is King. The

---

3. Ibid.

book rejected the view of King Charles I that kings had a divine right which was above the law. When Rutherford wrote and published it in 1644, the English civil war was in progress. As a twentieth-century biographer of Rutherford wrote, "its significance goes far beyond the times in which it was written."[4] The same biographer noted, *"Lex Rex* is beyond doubt one of the ablest pleas in defense of a constitutional form of government which has yet been written, and it still holds its place as one of the few great works on political science that Scotland has produced."[5] The book was publicly burned at Edinburgh in 1660, and Rutherford was accused of treason by Charles II who returned as monarch in that year, but died before trial.

Rutherford's view was that the laws given by God apply to everyone, including the rulers of countries. Human legislation should relate to the stated permanent laws of God, and be considered valid only if it is in agreement. This principle is the real alternative to the variable human consensus, and the arbitrary opinions of monarchs and totalitarian political parties. The current constitutional monarchy of Britain resulted in part from the case made out by Rutherford. *Lex Rex* was sensational and widely-read when published, and combined scholarly argument with what has been called "the passion of a Puritan and a patriot."

In simple terms, human behavior may be regulated by the consensus of other human beings only on the ground of human preference. The only principle involved is the power to enforce the will of whoever decides the law. Unfortunately, as we have seen, this will always lead to cases of plain injustice in all human systems of law. *If there is no reason for existing, there is equally no reason for behaving in any particular way.* What is missing is the essential link between our existence and our obligations. Such a link is possible only if we all owe our lives to a personal creator who has laid down the rules for our behavior.

Let us take a look at two statements of God's law. One is an abbreviated list of the ten commandments given directly by God in the Hebrew Bible, and the other is the summary of the law given by Jesus in response to a question about which commandment was the greatest. Here they are, in two little tables:

4. Loane, *Makers of Religious Freedom*, 78.
5. Ibid., 79.

Right and wrong

	THE TEN COMMANDMENTS	COMMENT
1	Have no other gods	Laws about your relationship with your heavenly Father
2	Have no images or idols	
3	Do not dishonor God's name	
4	Keep one day in seven for rest	Laws in your own interest to help you
5	Respect your parents	
6	Do not murder	Laws about how you should treat other people
7	Do not commit adultery	
8	Do not steal	
9	Do not tell lies about others	
10	Do not crave what is not yours	A law to help you think right

	JESUS' SUMMARY OF THE LAW
1	Love God with all your heart, soul, mind and strength
2	Love other people as if they were you yourself

The ten commandments

You will notice that I have divided the ten commandments into four groups. First come the laws about your relationship with God. The first of these is a simple statement that we are not to serve anyone else. Secondly, though we may think we put God first, we are told not to do anything which might *lead* us to break the first commandment. Human beings are all too capable of giving first place to things like sports or possessions, or even to other human beings who are our heroes. And the third commandment is important for those who claim to serve the true God: their actions should be consistent with their known beliefs. This will of course include not using God's name as a swear word, but that is only part of the meaning of this command.

The next two commandments are primarily to benefit those who keep them. Jesus said the Sabbath, the Jewish day of rest, was made for man, not man for the Sabbath. God intends us to have a special day of rest when we can pay special attention to him as well. In Christian times, the special day became Sunday, the first day of the week, to mark the day when Jesus rose from the dead. This is a time when we can really celebrate the greatness of our God. Such a God deserves celebrating, and it can be fun for us too!

The command to honor or respect our parents is a law to support family life, which in the New Testament is further supported by commands to parents and children. In this day and age there are many, like myself, who have had an unstable childhood through separation and divorce of parents, but that is no reason why we cannot have a good family life with our children. In fact, my wife and I view our children, and their spouses and children, as one of our greatest blessings from God.

The sixth to ninth commandments are related to law as it is known in most countries today. Murder (as distinct from killing which may be justifiable, for instance, in time of war), stealing and perjury find a place in most legal codes, but adultery may seem an odd prohibition in a society which often treats it as a joke, although it may of course be a legal ground for divorce. The reason it is singled out in these commandments is that it is a particularly nasty form of theft. A husband or wife who cheats is stealing from his or her partner, damaging the commitment which forms the base of marriage, and harming any children they may have. If the person with whom they cheat their partner is also married, two families are hurt.

Finally, envy or covetousness is forbidden. Why? Because it forms the motive for so many other law-breakings. Greed is undesirable, but envy elevates greed to a religion, with the second commandment broken in the process. As we shall see, God's ideal for us is the very opposite of greed, though it does not prevent us having many of this world's enjoyments.

Jesus' summary of God's law

In response to a question,[6] Jesus quoted two important items from the *extended* version of laws given in the second to fifth books of the Bible: Exodus, Leviticus, Numbers and Deuteronomy. First, from Deuteronomy 6:4–5 he quoted the "Shema" (the Hebrew word is from the opening words before the commandment, "Hear"), giving the very interesting *law* that the most important thing we can ever do is to *love* God. Why should we love God? First, because he is the creator of ourselves and all that we enjoy; secondly, because he is the person who has made provision for our forgiveness

6. Matt 22:34–40.

and reconciliation after we have rebelled against him; thirdly, because he wants us to be like he is: he gives his love freely and wants us to spread the idea that this is the only way to live.

What is love? In our world, the word has been debased. There are several aspects to real love; it is not mere longing or heartfelt desire; it is certainly not to be equated with sexual lust, although sex is a marvelous gift which God has given us to enjoy. The very best in love is giving, and not just giving, but giving the absolute essence of ourselves and all that we possess. Jesus said that the most loving thing anyone could do was to die for others,[7] and of course, that was what he did.

Jesus went further than endorsing the command to love God, and added his second command[8] that we should love other people. This seems to be easier to do than the first command; how can we love God whom we have not seen? Well, if we do *not* love God, we definitely shall not love other people. The reason is that if we are not in touch with God, we do not even *know* what is in other people's best interest. Only by understanding our creator, and by wanting to do what he says, can we help others. Because he loves the people he has created, loving him goes with loving other people. For us, these two commandments cannot exist separately.

The first principle of ethics: love God

Now, perhaps, we may begin to understand how important it is to be followers of Jesus Christ. Without him, we are destined to be wrong in our thinking and wrong in our behavior, however hard we may try to do what we think is right. There is a principle of perversity in our lives which prevents the best and often causes the worst to result from our actions. This plays a part in all of life, from our own personal actions to collective actions such as politics. The great philosopher Aristotle rightly perceived politics as an extension of ethics.

If we love God, we seek to know what he has said for our benefit, and to follow what he commands. At best we try to follow his example as Jesus showed it to us. If we do not love God, we reject any idea of his communicating with us, and we make up rules according to our own preference. At worst, we are the opposite of loving towards other human beings and seek to serve our own greed.

7. John 15:13.
8. from Lev 19:18.

The second principle of ethics: be forgiving

Jesus told a story about a man who was forgiven an enormous debt which he could never have repaid to his master. The man then threw into prison someone who owed him a comparatively tiny amount. When the master heard about it, he was angry and re-imposed the first man's debt with all its consequences. Jesus used the story to warn his followers that forgiveness of others was not just optional, but mandatory in view of what God had forgiven them.[9]

This is perhaps the most important way in which Christian behavior, truly understood, should differ from that of any other people. Almost every day it seems that we hear about some unforgiving act in the world we live in. The tit-for-tat of terrorism and mere reprisals needs to be distinguished from the just national and international rooting out of those who commit the most savage atrocities in a way that prevents them from doing it again. Tit-for-tat relates more to "an eye for an eye and a tooth for a tooth."

This principle of reciprocate damage given in the Hebrew Bible (an eye for an eye and a tooth for a tooth) was in fact a *limitation* of damage. Instead of being allowed to kill someone who harmed you, you were not allowed to do more to him than he had to you. It was a principle of *justice*, not an encouragement to hurt the offender. Jesus limited this further. Whilst not rejecting justice, Jesus encouraged us to forgive people.[10] This is one thing meant by loving other people. When people say, "I could never forgive him for what he did," they thereby risk not being forgiven themselves.

Forgiveness and love

The reason why I have proposed forgiveness as the second principle of ethics is that people so often overlook or ignore this excellent option, and you cannot really love God without forgiving people. Clearly, it is not possible to show such love when we forget how much God has forgiven those who want to follow him. It shows an awareness of our great debt to God as well as a desire to change the world by love. In the example I have quoted above from Jesus, we should note the circumstances. The persons who had offended sought forgiveness or at least some alleviation of the pressure to pay.

---

9. Matt 18:21–35.
10. Matt 6:14–5.

It was not a situation of national or international concern, where there may be principles of common justice to satisfy.

The Christian principle of forgiveness was clearly demonstrated by the sad events in a small town called Nickel Mines in Pennsylvania in October 2006.[11] A man called Charles Roberts went into a one-room Amish school and took ten girls hostage. Amish are pacifist Christians who take Christ's commands to his followers extremely seriously. Later, he shot all ten, five dying as a result, before shooting himself.

The evening of the same day, some Amish men went to visit the wife and children of the killer, and another went to the home of his parents. Their mission was to express their sorrow for these relatives and their total forgiveness of the killings. Other Amish people, asked whether they had anger in the following days, unanimously expressed forgiveness for the killer. When Roberts was buried a few days later, more than half the mourners at his funeral were Amish. When asked how they decided so quickly to extend forgiveness, some Amish laughed. An Amish bishop explained that it was spontaneous and automatic, a decided issue, not a new kind of thing.

Forgiveness and the state

Forgiveness does not rule out the principle of public justice. Indeed, although they are strict pacifists, the Amish believe that the state should maintain order, and justice is a part of that duty. As an example of this Christian belief in Britain, it is apparent that Myra Hindley, one of the notorious "moors murderers" in 1965, later became a Christian, repented of her actions, and asked God and the relatives of those she had harmed for forgiveness. This did not automatically mean she should be released from prison, where she died in 2002.

God has given the state a special role in managing both national and international affairs. The apostle Paul refers to the state as something which rightly should maintain law and justice. He used his status as a Roman citizen to claim justice when it was denied him.[12] The apostle Peter wrote that Christians should honor the king, probably at a time when the emperor Nero was persecuting Christians.[13]

---

11. Kraybill et al. *Amish Grace*.
12. e.g., Acts 22:25.
13. 1 Pet 2:17, perhaps using the word *king* from Prov 24:21.

Of course it is important to say that persecution is wrong. At the time of writing, there is violent and savage persecution of Christians in several countries, including Nigeria and Pakistan. This is as wrong as it would be to torture and kill members of another religion in Britain simply because they followed it. There was frequent discrimination against Christians in the former Communist countries of eastern Europe. But government is essential for maintenance of order in human affairs, and to that end it should be respected.

This was no easy option for Christians in New Testament times, nor is it today. Frequently it means working out precisely what the Christian may do without dishonoring God, when a state applies new pressures. In his first letter, Peter makes it quite plain that a Christian may suffer for serving Jesus Christ, but should never risk suffering by committing a crime. When there is no established order in a country, or an order imposed by a violent government as in Nazi Germany, there sometimes can be great difficulty in choosing what to do.

Jesus' further step in ethics

In the famous Sermon on the Mount, Jesus gave several examples of how Christian behavior should commend God to people. At the same time, he made it clear how impossible it was for us to obey God fully even when we wanted to. For instance, he advised giving *extra* help to persons who forced us to help them.[14] And he pointed out that a person could be an adulterer by intent, even though not by act.[15]

This expansion of the meaning of law is enough to humble anyone. God's standard is perfection, because he is perfect. When we understand just how far-reaching is God's command to be perfect, we begin to realize just how very imperfect and defective our own behavior is. Why should we try to be perfect? Because God originally made human beings perfect to share in the joy of his perfect creation. Jesus tells us to be perfect in the same Sermon on the Mount.[16] Since God is perfect, the nearer we approach his standard of behavior, the happier we shall be.

There is a story about an old Scottish lady who confided in the minister of her church one day that she had not sinned for three whole years. The

14. Matt 5:41.
15. Matt 5:28.
16. Matt 5:48.

minister was what the Scots would call a very canny man, and his response was: "Three whole years? You must be very proud of that!" The lady smiled and said, "Aye, I am that!" Even when we think we stand, we need to take care in case we fall. Perfection is not something we can achieve this side of physical death.

Why did Jesus die?

It is only when we realize how defective our behavior must seem to the perfect God who made us that we can understand why Jesus, God the Son, and therefore perfect, had to die to save us. People often ask why this particular act was necessary to bring us salvation. It seems very drastic for God to suffer in this way to bring us back to the hope of perfection in eternity. Indeed, followers of Islam consider it unthinkable that Jesus died, and they call him a prophet only, as they do not think he is God the Son.

First, we must point out that what Jesus did had to be understandable to his contemporaries. In his letter to the Christians in Galatia, Paul wrote[17] that Christ came at exactly the right time in history. It was a time when the rule of the Roman Empire meant that there was a common language—Greek—and the news of Jesus Christ could travel very easily over much of the civilized world on well-established routes. Jesus came to a nation—the Jews—who had been prepared over hundreds of years for his coming, by prophecy which he then proceeded to fulfill. His actions had to be in keeping with everything which God had done in that nation over the centuries.

The Jews had been taught at the time of Moses, the person who received the law from God, that an elaborate sacrificial system was necessary to approach God. There were several different ceremonies all revolving around the fact we have just considered, namely that God's perfection is far removed from our imperfection. One type of sacrificial offering was known as the sin offering. It was to allow for reconciliation of a repentant person to friendship with God, and forgiveness.

In the New Testament, it becomes clear that the sin offering itself was inadequate, and as Paul writes, the law could not literally achieve reconciliation, but was a *teacher* to show us how much we needed a *perfect* offering instead. The animals offered in the Old Testament provision were as near perfect as possible, but that was only a sign, not the reality. Some of the

---

17. Gal 4:4.

prophecies of Jesus in the Old Testament, particularly in the prophecy of Isaiah, are that the Christ is to be a sin offering.[18] How was this done?

In the New Testament it is shown that Jesus had to die, not simply physically, though that was a terrible ordeal, but *spiritually*. In a way we cannot fully comprehend, God the Son was spiritually separated from God the Father and the Holy Spirit when he died on the cross. What this meant for God the super-person in terms of suffering, no man can imagine. Just before he died on the cross, Jesus cried out, "My God, my God, why have you forsaken me?"[19] He was quoting the first sentence of Psalm 22 in the Old Testament, a psalm which quite amazingly describes the agony of the crucifixion, *perhaps a thousand years before it actually happened*. Only as God the Son, and therefore man as well as God, could Jesus experience the full agony of separation from the Father.

Could God have done it differently?

When people appreciate just how far-reaching the death of Jesus was, they sometimes ask, "Why? Isn't God great enough to have done it some other way? Couldn't he simply forgive us without sending Jesus?" When we ask such questions, they are usually a result of our thinking that it is unfair for Jesus to suffer on our behalf. Perhaps it was possible for God to act in some other way, but not with full regard to all he intended to achieve.

His purpose was to restore to us all that he had first given us. In the history which actually developed in his creation following the fall of humankind, God's new gift was even more demanding on him than the first. He intended to show us that our disobedience was *not* something which could be forgiven lightly, and to that end, he suffered unimaginably. His love for us had a significant cost for him.

God doesn't tell us simply to be good, but he makes us good if we want him to

The message which the Bible presents to us is that we cannot in any way restore ourselves to harmony with the God against whom we have offended. No amount of trying to do good is able to achieve this reconciliation. What

---

18. e.g., Is 53:4–12.
19. Matt 27:46.

Right and wrong

it needs is the sacrifice—the gift—of a totally *perfect* entity. Only God could fit this requirement, and he therefore was born as a human being in order to do so. His perfection, in a way that he had planned, allowed us to be changed so that eventually, after this life is over, we may be restored to perfection. But there is a further bonus. If we ask his forgiveness here and now, we are restored to friendship with him here and now.

So where do morals come in? If we cannot achieve perfection in this life, we still have two benefits. One is that we know how God wants us to behave, and the other is that we may have his help. At last we are set free to make his desires our objectives, and we may begin to love him, albeit imperfectly. A tremendous change is possible in our lives, and the future begins to look different and better.

But what if we do not want this? Will God interfere with our desire to be left alone and not bothered by him? Are we not adults and capable of making our own decisions? As I mentioned in chapter 18, to reject God is possible, but it is to accept hell, the absence of all that is good, because all good has its origin in God. Although in this life we are not cut off completely from God, that is a goal which is achievable; but it represents merely the culmination of living without him. If we truly seek something better, the only option is to ask him for the best which is available—restoration to eventual perfection.

Epilogue

Alpha and Omega

This is what the LORD says—Israel's King and Redeemer, the LORD Almighty: I am the first and I am the last; apart from me there is no God. (Isa 44:6, NIV.)

Do not be afraid. I am the First and the Last. I am the Living One; I was dead, and behold I am alive for ever and ever! (Rev 1:17–18, NIV.)

IN THE WORLD WE see around us, death rules. Throughout the history of the earth, organisms beyond numbering have died physically. The earth, according to what we know of science, is doomed. So is the sun, so are the stars of our galaxy, the Milky Way, and so is the entire universe. And not surprisingly, people in this generation are beginning to take it on board. They say, "What is the point?" They question every morality, every supposed truth, and they behave as they want to.

God has put his signposts—his fingerprints—into our lives. If we look at this amazingly complex ordered universe, dominated by cause and effect, the first question to arise is "Why does anything exist?" This is not a question of mere *scientific* origins, for we can trace everything back to the big bang. We can answer part of the question, "How did this universe come to its present form?" No, the first question is of *absolutes*, of why there is something rather than nothing, order rather than chaos, and many layers of complexity within many types of unity, including why we are able to perceive, investigate and interact with our surroundings.

The next question arises from following these signposts. Because it is so clear that no one can see outside the universe from within, we have to look for messages from outside. This is not a weird science fiction quest, as in some modern religions. Nor is it a quest for a secret which is only open to a few super-brains. It is a quest to which we are all directed, whether we

Epilogue

are Nobel prize winners or learning-disabled. God is no respecter of differences in the capabilities of our brains, which in any case he made!

God's principle is of *life*, a life that is so powerful that it dominates what we see around us. He is a self-existent and complex person who is three persons in one—the Living God. Above, I have quoted two brief passages, previously referred to in chapter 20. The first is from the Hebrew Bible, known to Christians as the Old Testament. In it, the prophet Isaiah states that God is a ruler, a savior, totally powerful and outside and greater than all he has created.

The second passage is from the last book of the New Testament, Revelation, an account of a vision given to a man who was persecuted and imprisoned on an island simply because he was a Christian. His vision starts with the terrifying glory of the figure of Jesus Christ, who claims to be the same Almighty God, the First and the Last, and who states that he *was* dead, but now lives for ever.

This is but one of the many clear pointers in the New Testament to the fact that Jesus is God. In the same book of Revelation, as in other parts of the New Testament, the Holy Spirit is also clearly a person. For instance he *speaks* to the symbolic churches in chapters 2 and 3, he brings visions (chapters 1 and 4), he is complete (the seven spirits) before the throne of the Father, as is Jesus who died as a sacrificial Lamb (chapters 4 and 5), and he moves the complete church of God (the bride of Jesus Christ) to yearn for the completion of human history (chapter 22).

For mere human beings, the Holy Trinity of God is too great for simple mathematical understanding. But God is the creator of mathematics and logic as well as everything else. He has given us clear indications that his personal being is both a unity and a complexity. Were he not in this form, he would not be self-sufficient as a person, he would not be love, and his personality would lack communication as an inbuilt characteristic. As it is, we can see that he is love, that he is greater than everything created in the universe, and he is totally self-sufficient without having to create the universe or anything else. Indeed, his creation and continual provision for its existence is one of his great acts of love. His communication to us is another, and his great salvation for us is another.

At the start of chapter 20, I also quoted the famous proverb, "The fear of the LORD is the beginning of wisdom, and knowledge of the Holy One is understanding."[1] In these few pages, we have looked at the simplicity of

---

1 Prov 9:10.

Epilogue

God's communication to us all. As is clear in that communication, he values humility above intellectual ability, and he wants us to show love to those around us, as he shows love to us. There is a future, and there is a purpose beyond this created universe. His life is powerful beyond our present understanding, and he actually encourages us to love him and relate to him. Not only do we find wisdom in recognizing and following his words, but we also find our complete fulfillment in them. As Jesus said, "I am the way, the truth and the life. No-one comes to the Father except through me."[2]

There is something significant to add in this book. In chapter 5, we looked at the ways in which the earth or the universe might come to an end. This is only according to the projections of science, and if they are true, then ultimately there is no basis for human ethics, as we have discussed. However, the revelation of the triune God in the Christian Bible includes one significant prediction of the future. At a time which human beings cannot predict, the Lord of all history—Jesus—will return to this earth and bring everything to a close, and then to a new beginning. As far as the Bible can be understood, Jesus will return, all humanity will be raised from the dead, unless they live till he comes, and a final judgment of everyone will take place.[3] The last chapters of the Bible contain a clear statement that there will be a new heaven *and a new earth*,[4] and the implication of the whole of scripture is that those who are God's people will then have the joyful existence which God intended for us before sin intervened and led to the disastrous moral state of our planet now.

For the present, we may find it hard to understand that our universe is only part of the big picture. Once we adopt the right perspective through seeking and listening to God's messages to us, things begin to fall into place. This is only the beginning. There is a life full of meaning ahead.

---

2 John 14:6.
3 e.g., 2 Pet 3:1–14; 1 Cor 15:51–57; 1 Thess 4:14—5:11.
4 Rev 21:1.

Bibliography

Alexander, Denis. *Rebuilding the Matrix. Science and Faith in the 21st Century.* Oxford: Lion Publishing, 2001.
Anglican Curmudgeon. "*Dennis Canon loses in South Carolina.*" No pages. Online: http://accurmudgeon.blogspot.co.uk/2009/09/dennis-canon-loses-in-south-carolina.html.
——— "*Episcopal Church (USA)—the Spoiled Child of the Anglican Communion—Wants It All.*" Online: http://accurmudgeon.blogspot.co.uk/2012/07/episcopal-church-usa-spoiled-child-of.html.
Ashworth, Lorna. "Background Paper. That this Synod express the desire that the Church of England be in communion with the Anglican Church in North America." London: General Synod of the Church of England, 2009. Online: http://www.churchofengland.org/media/39109/gs1764a.pdf.
Baggini, Julian. *Atheism. A Very Short Introduction.* Oxford: Oxford University Press, 2003.
Barrett, Stephen. *Quackwatch.* Online: http://quackwatch.com.
Baughen, Michael A. *The One Big Question. The God of Love in a World of Suffering.* Farnham, Surrey: CWR, 2010.
BBC News. "Final blow for Hanratty family." July 4, 2002. No pages. Online: http://news.bbc.co.uk/1/hi/wales/2093650.stm.
———. "Three freed as St Paul's trial collapses." May 24, 2002. No pages. Online: http://news.bbc.co.uk/1/hi/england/2006151.stm.
——— "Climbie killer says sorry." January 30, 2002. No pages. Online: http://news.bbc.co.uk/1/hi/england/1792336.stm.
——— "Climbie killer disrupts enquiry." January 8, 2002. No pages. Online: http://news.bbc.co.uk/1/hi/england/1748718.stm.
Berry, R. J. *God and Evolution.* London: Hodder & Stoughton, 1988.
——— "Rejection of the Creator." In *Caring for Creation. Biblical and theological perspectives,* 39–45. Oxford: BRF, 2005.
Blocher, Henri. *In the Beginning. The opening chapters of Genesis.* Leicester: Inter-Varsity Press, 1984.
Board on Physics and Astronomy. *Revealing the Hidden Nature of Space and Time: Charting the Course for Elementary Particle Physics.* Washington DC: National Academies Press, 2006. Online: http://www.nap.edu/catalog.php?record_id=11641.
Brown, Colin. *Philosophy and the Christian Faith. A Historical Sketch from the Middle Ages to the Present Day.* London: Tyndale Press, 1969.
Brown, Wilfred. *Organization.* London: Heinemann, 1971.
Bruce, Frederic F. *The New Testament Documents. Are they Reliable?* 6th ed. Grand Rapids: Eerdmans, 1981.
Carey, George, and Andrew Carey. *We Don't Do God. The marginalization of public faith.* Oxford: Monarch Books, 2012.

Bibliography

Carson, Rachel. *Silent Spring*. Boston: Houghton Mifflin, 1962.
Chang, Jung, and Jon Halliday. *Mao. The Unknown Story*. London: Jonathan Cape, 2005.
Darwin Awards, 1997. "More Darwin Award candidates." No pages. Online: http://www.searchablejokes.com/jdarwin.htm.
Dostoevsky, Fyodor. *The Idiot*. No pages. Online: http://www.online-literature.com/dostoevsky/idiot/2/.
Egger. M., et al. "Spurious precision? Meta-analysis of observational studies." *BMJ* 316 (1998) 140–144.
Emsley, John. *The Shocking History of Phosphorus. A biography of the Devil's element*. London: Macmillan, 2000.
Esper, J, et al. "Climate in northern Europe reconstructed for the past 2,000 years: Cooling trend calculated precisely for the first time." No pages. Online: http://www.uni-mainz.de/eng/15491.php.
Fox, Robin L. *The Unauthorized Version. Truth and Fiction in the Bible*. London: Penguin Books, 1991.
French, Richard V. (editor) *Lex Mosaica. The Law of Moses and the Higher Criticism*. London: Eyre and Spottiswoode, 1894.
Gardner, Rex. "Miracles of healing in Anglo-Celtic Northumbria as recorded by the Venerable Bede and his contemporaries: a reappraisal in the light of twentieth century experience." *BMJ* 287 (1983) 1927–33.
Groat, Joel, B. " Changes to Latter-day Scripture: LDS Leaders Have Made Thousands of Changes to Mormon Scriptures — Why?" No pages. Online: http://www.irr.org/mit/changing-scripture.html.
Heschel, Susannah. *The Aryan Jesus. Christian Theologians and the Bible in Nazi Germany*. Princeton: Princeton University Press, 2008.
Hexham, Irving. *Understanding World Religions*. Grand Rapids: Zondervan, 2011.
Hillerbrand, Hans J. *The Reformation in its Own Words*. London: SCM Press, 1964.
Hitchens, Peter. *The Rage against God*. London, UK: Continuum Books, 2010.
Hoffman, Banesh. *The Strange Story of the Quantum*. Harmondsworth, Middlesex: Penguin Books, 1963.
Hopper, Kenneth, and William Hopper. *The Puritan Gift. Triumph, Collapse and Revival of an American Dream*. London: I.B.Tauris, 2007.
Horton, R. "A statement by the editors of The Lancet." *Lancet* 363 (2004) 820–21.
Hume, David. *A Treatise of Human Nature*. Harmondsworth, Middlesex: Penguin Books, 1969.
Kahn, Herman. *On Thermonuclear War*. Princeton: Princeton University Press, 1960.
Kiefer, James E. "Polycarp, Bishop of Smyrna and Martyr." No pages. Online: http://justus.anglican.org/resources/bio/108.html.
Kitchen, Kenneth A. *Ancient Orient and Old Testament*. London: Tyndale Press, 1966.
——— *On the Reliability of the Old Testament*. Grand Rapids: Eerdmans, 2003.
Kraybill, Donald B., et al. *Amish Grace. How Forgiveness Transcended Tragedy*. San Francisco: Jossey-Bass, 2010.
Lewis, C. S. *Mere Christianity*, London: Collins, 1952.
——— "The Humanitarian Theory of Punishment." In *Churchmen Speak. Thirteen Essays*. Abingdon, Berkshire, UK: Marcham Manor, 1966, 39–44.
Loane, Marcus L. *Makers of Religious Freedom in the Seventeenth Century. Henderson. Rutherford. Bunyan. Baxter*. London: Intervarsity Fellowship, 1960.
Martin, Walter R. *The Kingdom of the Cults*. Grand Rapids: Zondervan, 1965.

Bibliography

Montgomery, John W. *The Suicide of Christian Theology*. Newbergh: Trinity Press, 1970.
Moore, Patrick, et al. *Atlas of the Solar System*, London: Mitchell Beazley, 1983.
Morison, Frank. *Who Moved the Stone?* London: Faber and Faber, 1958.
National Maritime Museum, "The Universe." No pages. Online: http://www.rmg.co.uk/explore/astronomy-and-time/astronomy-facts/universe/cosmology.
Pearce, E.K Victor. *Who was Adam?* Exeter: Paternoster, 1969.
Penrose, Roger. *Cycles of Time. An Extraordinary New View of the Universe*. London: Vintage Books, 2011.
Quran. No pages. Online: http://www.islamicity.com/mosque/QURAN/5.htm.
Rees, Martin. *Just Six Numbers. The Deep Forces that Shape the Universe*. London: Weidenfeld & Nicholson, 1999.
Robinson, John A. T. *Redating the New Testament*. Eugene, OR: Wipf and Stock, 2000.
Ruse, Michael. "Dawkins et al bring us into disrepute." *The Guardian*, November 2, 2009. No pages. Online: http://www.guardian.co.uk/commentisfree/belief/2009/nov/02/atheism-dawkins-ruse
Schaeffer, Francis A. *He is There and He is not Silent*. London: Hodder & Stoughton, 1972.
Smolin, Lee. *Three Roads to Quantum Gravity*. London: Weidenfeld & Nicholson, 2000.
Speiser, E.A., translator. "The Creation Epic." In *Ancient Near Eastern Texts Relating to the Old Testament*. 3rd ed., 60–72. Edited by James B. Pritchard. Princeton: Princeton University Press, 1969.
Thiele, Edwin R. *The Mysterious Numbers of the Hebrew Kings*. Grand Rapids: Eerdmans, 1965.
Wenham, John. *Easter Enigma*. Exeter: Paternoster,1984.
Whitcomb, John C. Jr., and Henry M. Morris. *The Genesis Flood. The Biblical Record and its Scientific Implications*. Philadelphia: Presbyterian and Reformed, 1961.
Wikipedia. "*Dennis Canon*." No pages. Online: http://en.wikipedia.org/wiki/Dennis_Canon.
Wilson, David M. *The Bayeux Tapestry*. London: Thames & Hudson, 2004.

Subject/Name Index

addiction, 18
agreement, 22, 61, 111, 122, 140, 166, 184
agnosticism 3, 118, 148
   humility of, 3
agriculture (see *farming*)
Albania, 156
Alexander, Denis, 11–12, 149, 199
Amish Christians, 189, 200
antimatter, 80
arbitrariness, 38–39, 110, 120, 135, 159
archaeology, 6–7, 154, 173
   evidence of, 6–7, 143–44, 170–75
Archimedes ("Archimedean point"), 120
arts,
   literary, 42, 87, 93
   visual, 42, 50, 67, 85, 92
   music, 42, 50, 67, 87, 93, 99, 112, 128–29
assumption (see also *axiom* and *presupposition*), 3, 24, 33, 50–51, 60, 92, 98, 119
atheism,
   arrogance of, 3
   faith of, 4, 18, 112–13, 117–19
   no evidence for, 3–5, 118
   irrationality of, 3, 5, 12, 18, 118
   Marxist, 4, 99
   mysticism of, 3–4, 118
   violence of, against Christianity, 4, 156, 190
Attenborough, Sir David 97, 151
   and ethics, 130
axiom (see also *assumption* and *presupposition*), 24, 33, 119, 139
Aztecs, 111
Ba'athist regime, 31
Baggini, Julian, 5–6, 199

bar-Kochba, Simon, 84, 143
Baudelaire, Charles Pierre, 114
Baughen, Michael, 159, 199
Bayeux Tapestry, 6–7, 201
behavior and education, 181
Bible
   accuracy of, 8, 144, 169–71
   consistency with naïve experience of, 166–69
   external consistency of, 6–7, 143–44, 170–79
   internal consistency of, 169–72
   views of Jesus on, 143–44, 165–66
boson, force-carrying, 66–67, 74, 101–2, 113, 150–51
brane (physics), 102
Bruce, Frederic Fyvie, 8, 144, 199
brute force, 11, 39, 105, 110
Carey, Andrew, 10, 199
Carey, George, 10, 199
Carson, Rachel, 43, 50, 200
causation (see also *uniformity of natural causes*), 26, 80–86
chance, 18–19, 58, 74, 95
chaos, 23–24, 27, 47, 63, 69–70, 146, 195
   non-existence of, 74–79
   theory, 63
Christianity,
   evidence-based, 13–14, 117–27
   evangelical,
      religious persecution of, 9–10
      secular persecution of, 10
   good deeds and, 57, 125–26, 133
   liberal,
      anti-Semitism of, 9
      intolerance of, 10
      un-Biblical behavior, of 9
chronology, 170–71

Subject/Name Index

church, Christian, 67, 84, 115, 142–43, 145, 154, 159, 169, 171–72, 196
classification, 25, 40, 50, 89, 93, 102, 120
commitment, 29–31, 152, 186
communication, 50, 52, 63, 71, 86, 89, 94, 96–105, 109, 114, 121, 174, 196–97
   and information, 96–105
complexity, 11, 41–2, 65–67, 73, 74–78, 82, 95, 101, 112–13, 124–25, 146–47, 150–51, 168–69
   on complexity, 101–4
Confessing Church, 9
Conquest, Norman, of England, 6–7
consistency, 19–20, 34, 45–48, 52, 140
   as check on truth, 162–79
constants, physical, 11
   particles and 150–51
control, 30–31, 43, 50, 53, 66, 68, 73, 77–79, 85, 87, 99, 105, 110–11, 133, 158, 160
conversion, personal, 146–54, 156–58
creation, as origin of all, 11–12, 71, 75, 112–116, 121–27, 135–36, 144, 163–68
creationism, "fiat", 11–12, 75, 163, 173
criticism, "higher", 8–9, 200
death, 5, 17, 24, 33, 34, 60, 65, 69, 76, 115, 123, 159–60, 175, 195
   of Jesus, 141–43, 157–58, 168, 192
   penalty, 32, 100, 126, 131, 182
decision,
   arbitrary, 38
   committee, 73, 182
   rational or evidence-based, 50, 72–73, 92–93, 120, 131, 135, 137, 156–61
deterrence (of criminals), 31, 182–83
Deuteronomy, date of, 7
dimension (physics), 34–35, 40–41, 81, 102, 110
disabled people,
   brain-damaged, 93
   deaf-blind, 27
   learning-disabled, 196
disagreement, 14, 57, 60, 119, 122, 139, 164, 171

Dostoevsky, Fyodor, 131, 200
Earth, end of, 35–36, 197
electron, 66, 80, 165
Enlightenment, the, 30
entropy, 65
ethics,
   and consensus, 180–84
   and facts, 32–33, 130–31, 151–52
   atheist, 4, 14
   death of, 110
   foundations of, 14, 68, 135–36
   personal source for, 14, 135–36
   postmodern, 9–10
   preference, 4, 6, 13–14, 37–38, 104, 110–12, 151–52, 183–84
   principles of Christian, 183–91
   "survival of fittest", 14
evidence, 3–9, 13, 18, 51, 57–61, 66–67, 72–73, 83–85, 89, 102–3, 105, 109, 113, 117–19, 126, 138–39, 143–44, 147, 166–79, 181
evil, 72, 91, 98, 110–11, 113–14, 120, 122, 126, 128–36, 144–45, 160–61, 167, 177–79
evolution, 10–12, 75, 102–3, 141, 149, 177
   as history rather than origin, 11–12, 75, 141
   natural selection in, 102–3
   random genetic mutation in, 69, 103
experiment, 22, 24, 35, 46, 48, 51, 54, 55–56, 59, 62, 66, 92, 102–3, 121, 127, 139–40, 146, 163–64
farming, 33, 43–44, 50
   "organic", 33, 43–44
Florida, legal aspects of, 38, 131
forgiveness, 122, 157, 161, 186, 188–93
force, brute (see *brute force*)
Fox, Robin Lane, 6–8, 200
framework, 40–48, 56–57, 59, 62, 68, 93, 139–40, 142, 165, 175–76
Galton, Sir Francis, 24
German Christian movement, 9
global warming, 33, 130
global cooling, 130
God,
   and words, 98

204

Subject/Name Index

image, of, 71, 168, 178
    relating to, 124–26, 132, 152, 197
gods,
    Babylonian (Akkadian), 111–12, 177–78
    Greek, 111–12, 122
    Hindu, 122, 125
Harvard MBA, 78–79
Hegel, Georg Wilhelm Friedrich, 6, 8
herbal medicine, 44
Heschel, Susannah, 9, 200
history,
    essential truths, 141
    objective reference points, 100, 170
Hitchens, Christopher, 4
Hitchens, Peter, 4, 200
Hitler, Adolph, 9, 32, 111
Holy Spirit, 8, 115–16, 123, 144, 165, 173, 192, 196
    divinity and personality of, 8, 123–25, 168
Holy Trinity, 8, 124–25, 135, 152, 158, 167, 196
homeopathy, 44
Hopper, Kenneth and William, 78–79, 200
Humanist religion, 130, 159
Hume, David, 21, 200
Huxley, Thomas Henry, 3
ice age, 33, 130
identity, 17, 52, 71, 86–95, 114, 120, 134, 136, 146, 149
information, 50–51, 74, 101–4
    and communication, 96–97
Islam, 14, 121–22, 147, 180, 191
    critical discussion of, 126
    impossibility of discussing truth of, 126
Jesus Christ, 5, 8–9, 84, 123–26, 129, 133–36, 143–44, 152, 165–66, 168–69,181–97
    anger of, 159–60
    death of, 67, 115, 125, 141–42, 149–50, 157–58, 191–92, 196
    divinity of, 115, 123–25, 134, 168
    relating to, 154, 158, 161

resurrection of, 66–67, 84, 142–43, 149–50, 171–72, 186
    evidence for, 84, 142–43
    summary of God's law by, 184–87
Judaïsm, 7, 14, 121–25, 147
justice, 10, 32, 59, 100, 131, 157, 160, 183–84, 188–89
Kitchen, Kenneth A., 7, 174, 200
Kittel, Gerhard, 9
law, 9, 14, 19–20, 30–31, 38–39, 52, 120, 122, 129, 133, 135, 137, 151, 157, 160, 165, 167, 180-191
    and anarchy, 19
    variations in, 38
    human opinions on, 37–38, 181–82
    human preferences, for 110, 120, 152, 180–83
    scientific, 5, 45–46, 51, 54, 58, 65, 67–68, 70, 76–77, 79, 81, 85, 114, 150–51, 176–77
Leibniz, Gottfried Wilhelm, 22
lepton 66–67, 74, 101–2, 113, 150–51
Lessing, Gotthold (Lessing's Ditch), 58–59, 72
Lex Rex, 183–84
limits, 17, 34–38
    implications, of 37–38
love, 4, 29, 39, 67, 96, 115–16, 120, 122, 124, 127, 129, 142, 147, 152, 154, 156–59, 167–68, 185–88, 192–93, 196–97
    and ethics, 185–89
    and human need, 95
Luke, historical accuracy, of 8
Luther, Martin, 129, 133
Mao Tse-Tung, 14, 200
marriage, 29, 177, 186
matter-energy, 81, 83, 102
memory, 27, 49, 89, 91–92, 101, 114, 120
Milligan, Spike, 69, 73
miracles, 12, 52, 66–67, 72, 80–86, 144
    of healing, 82–84
    space-time discontinuity of, 84–85, 143–44
    of Jesus, 84, 123, 142, 160
MMR (measles, mumps and rubella) vaccine scandal, 60–61

Subject/Name Index

monasticism, 129–30
Moon landing, 36, 142
Morris, Henry M., 12, 201
multiverse (see *universe, multiple*)
murderers, 100, 131
    moors, 37, 189
naïve experience, 1, 22–28, 33, 48, 50–54, 56, 60–62, 67–69, 89, 100–2, 104, 116, 117–21, 135, 137, 138–40, 144, 156, 166–69
    interpretation of, 101
National Health Service (NHS), UK, 78–79
Nazis, 9, 88, 190
Napoleon, 7
neutron, 66
order, 17, 23–25, 27, 40, 52, 54, 56, 58, 63, 65, 68, 73, 74–79, 81, 85, 89, 93, 104, 112, 120, 135, 137, 140, 146–47, 156, 167, 195
    and chaos, 23, 27, 74, 146
    "disorder", 27–28, 63, 65, 76–79, 91
origins, 12, 18, 26, 101, 109–16, 119, 121, 136, 141–42, 146–47, 155, 157, 165, 167, 177, 193, 195
    creation, 12, 75, 178
    of universe, 52, 120, 164, 176, 177
    of persons, 14, 18, 81, 107, 138
pantheism, 98, 109, 113–14, 120
    "paneverythingism", 109, 120
perfection,
    as a Christian aim, 190–91, 193
    desire for, 94, 102, 120
persecution, 4, 143, 156, 172, 190
personality, 14, 17–18, 71, 87–95, 102–3, 109–16, 119–20, 124, 125, 147, 177
philosophy, 1, 4–6, 16, 35, 46, 48, 50, 53, 58, 68, 99, 140, 177
    and human history, 48, 58, 60, 140, 177
Positivism, self-destruction of, 47, 99
Postmodernism, 1, 10
    intolerance of, 10
    manipulation ethic of, 9–10
    self-destruction of, 47
presupposition (see also *assumption* and *axiom*), 33, 72, 119, 139
probability, 15, 150
proton, 36, 66
Proxima Centauri, 36
punishment, 89, 123, 142, 159, 161
    and morality, 182–83
    capital, 32, 100, 126, 131, 182
purity and profanity, 128–136
quark, 66–67, 74, 101–2, 113, 150–51
Rad, Gerhard von, 9
randomness, 68–70, 74, 103, 145
reason, 1, 4, 8, 13, 22, 45, 48, 49–54, 76, 85, 111, 118, 130, 182
    and experience, 55–62, 118–19, 137–45
    end of?, 137–38
Rees, Sir Martin, 11, 112, 201
reflection, 23, 50, 89, 92–3, 102, 120
reform (of criminals), 181–83
religions (and other philosophies of life), 4–5, 13, 15–16, 47, 82, 84, 89–90, 98–99, 111, 114, 117–27, 136, 147–49, 157–58, 167, 190
    of unbelief, 118–19, 157–59, 186
    minor, 121, 125, 130, 147, 149–50, 195
resurrection, 67, 84, 143–4, 150, 158, 168, 171–72
revelation, 14, 107, 121–24, 140–41, 174, 197
    natural, 121, 140
    special, 121–24, 136, 143–44, 147, 149, 165–69, 174, 197
    religions of, 121–27, 140, 143
right and wrong, 31–33, 39, 104, 179, 180–195
rights, 19, 30–31, 38
    and obligations, 30–31
risks, 44, 55, 60, 62, 70, 130, 134, 145, 188
Rosenberg, Alfred, 9
Rousseau, Jean-Jacques, 30–31
Rutherford, Samuel, 183–84
Sade, Marquis de, 31, 37, 120
Sartre, Jean-Paul, 23
Schaeffer, Francis, 109–10, 113, 119, 201

Subject/Name Index

sciences
  astronomy, 35–37, 41, 57, 61, 129, 170, 199, 201
  biology, 10–12, 14, 24, 41–43, 47, 49–50, 65, 74, 76–77, 85, 87, 93, 102–5, 130, 149, 151, 163, 173, 176–79
  chemistry, 11, 24, 33, 41–44, 65–66, 76–77, 78, 87, 90, 102, 104, 114, 129, 151, 176
  cosmology, 41, 82, 176
  medical, 44–45, 60–61, 68, 84, 93
  physics, 11, 34, 41, 45, 47, 54, 65, 67, 77, 79, 80–82, 85, 87, 101–2, 114, 120, 129, 150–52, 163, 176
  sociology, 38, 99–100, 163
self, 23, 26–27, 54, 56, 68, 71–72, 89–92, 104, 114–16, 124, 146
sequence, 17, 25, 27, 53–54, 56, 68, 72, 75, 80–86, 104, 137, 140, 146–47
shark, great white, 15
sin, 122–23, 135, 154, 161, 179, 190–92, 197
  and good works, 125–26
solipsism, 23, 26, 34–35, 47, 52, 89
Solzhenitsyn, Alexander, 38, 88, 133
something or nothing, 13, 22–23, 27, 51–52, 54, 65–73, 75, 101, 104, 109–10, 120–121, 144, 146, 150, 156, 164, 167, 176, 195
space, 34–39, 52–53, 76, 80, 91, 103
  travel through, 36–37, 112
  space-time, 17, 40–41, 46, 48, 53, 63, 71, 81, 116, 141, 176–78
    discontinuity, of 82–85, 143–44
state,
  role of, 189–90
  police, 13–14, 67–68, 105
  types of, 4, 13–14, 67–68, 105, 156
Stalin, 88, 133
storks, 26, 53
string (physics), 102
suffering, 38, 88, 94, 113, 141, 144–45, 158–59, 177, 190
  of God, 191–92
super-personality, 14, 109, 114–116, 117, 120, 123–125, 136, 152, 156, 161, 167–69, 192

  and love, 115, 152, 156, 168
technology, 42–44, 50, 112, 151, 181
Ten Commandments, 184–86
terrorists, 19, 27, 44, 105, 111, 139, 180, 188
time, 17, 25, 34–39, 40–42, 46, 48, 52–54, 56, 58, 63, 68, 71–72, 74, 80–85, 112, 116, 141–44, 146, 159, 176–78
Tiananmen Square massacre, 31
Tolkien, J.R.R., 128
trust, 18, 28, 29–33, 57, 61–62, 97, 139, 146, 149, 154, 178
truth
  and minor religions, 149–50
  literal, 163–65, 175–77
    different interpretations of, 163, 175
  metaphorical, 164–65
  scientific, 63–65
  types of, 162–65
tumor, 70, 103
unbelief, religion of, 118–19, 156
uniformity of natural causes, 46, 52, 80, 84–85, 118
unity and diversity, 25, 27, 40, 52, 54, 56, 63, 68, 104, 114, 124, 137, 140, 146–47
  and classification, 25
  and communication, 63, 104
  and God, 114, 116, 124, 147
universe,
  beginning of, 35–36, 52, 75, 77, 81, 113–14, 116, 120, 135–36, 147, 150, 163–64, 176–77
  end of, 4, 35–39, 69, 76, 110, 164, 197
  outside of, 3, 12–13, 82, 85–86, 96, 107, 118, 128
  multiple (multiverse), 11, 82, 105, 112–13
uniqueness, 8, 17, 49–50, 68, 70–72, 87–91, 122–23, 152, 177
void, the (non-being), 21, 69
Wellhausen, Julius, 6–9, 175
Whitcomb, John C Jr., 12, 201

www.ingramcontent.com/pod-product-compliance
Lightning Source LLC
Chambersburg PA
CBHW070338230426
43663CB00011B/2374